SUPER™ QAR

for Test-Wise Students

Student Activity Book

This book belongs to:

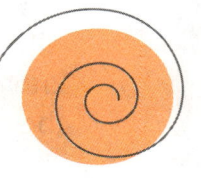

Wright Group

The McGraw·Hill Companies

Question Answer Relationships

In the Book

Right There

The answer is "right there" in the text. It is often a detail question.

Think and Search

The answer is in the text and involves cross-text searches. Identifying text structures such as the following helps organize your answer.

- Simple List
- Explanation
- Sequence
- Compare and Contrast
- Cause and Effect
- Problem and Solution

In My Head

Author and Me

The information to answer the question comes from background knowledge. You need to read the text and understand the question and you need to make connections.

- Text to Self: How the text affects the way you think or believe.
- Text to Text: Make connections with different texts you've read.
- Text to Themes: Use what you've read to generalize, identify themes, or interpret text.

On My Own

All the ideas and information to answer the question come from background knowledge, experiences, and beliefs. The question can be answered without reading the text.

Directions: Read this passage from *American History: The Early Years to 1877* by Donald A. Ritchie and Albert S. Broussard.

The Women's Rights Movement

Women took a special interest in the antislavery movement. As they fought for social reform for African Americans, they realized that they also lacked full social and political rights. When women tried to participate in the antislavery movement, they often met resistance. As a result, many abolitionists became crusaders for women's rights.

Equal rights for women would require major reform. In the 1800s women actually had fewer rights than in colonial times. They had few political or legal rights. Women could not vote or hold public office. A woman's husband owned all of her property.

Women from New England to Ohio joined the antislavery societies. Many saw similarities between the treatment of enslaved persons and women.

Journalist Margaret Fuller observed that "there exists in the minds of men a tone of feeling toward women as towards slaves." Abolitionists Angelina and Sarah Grimké confronted this feeling when they spoke to antislavery groups. Audiences did not criticize their stand on slavery. They did, though, question their right to speak in public.

As a result, the Grimkés soon found themselves in the midst of "an entirely new contest—a contest for the rights of woman." Sarah wrote that "all I ask… is that [men] will take their feet from off our necks and permit us to stand upright."

QAR Characteristics

IN THE BOOK

Right There

Source:

The answer is found in the text.

The answer is easily found within a single statement or paragraph.

Wording:

The wording of the question is found in the text and may be repeated in the answer.

The answer may use the exact wording in the text.

Content:

The answer is usually a definition, a fact, or a detail from the text.

Format:

The question-answer format is usually multiple-choice.

Think and Search

Source:

The answer is found in the text.

The answer is found in more than one statement, paragraph, or section of the text.

Wording:

The wording of the question may or may not be found in the text.

The answer may or may not use the wording in the text.

Content:

The answer may require inferring or summarizing from information given in the text.

The answer may address the main idea of the text.

Format:

The question-answer format may be multiple-choice or short answer.

IN MY HEAD

Author and Me

Source:

The answer is based on my own knowledge and experience.

The answer combines an understanding of the text with my own knowledge or experience. It may connect to other texts I have read.

Wording:

The wording of the question is unlikely to be found in the text.

The answer may or may not use wording in the text. The answer may refer to or draw on points made in the text.

Content:

The answer is a narrative inferred from or based on information given in the text.

The answer addresses the main idea or theme of the text.

Format:

The question-answer format may be multiple-choice, short answer, or extended response (essay).

On My Own

Source:

The answer is based on my own knowledge and experience.

The answer is independent of the text. It is related to the general topic of the text but comes from my own experience, knowledge, and reading.

Wording:

The wording of the question is not found in the text.

The answer will not use wording in the text.

Content:

The answer is a personal narrative (explanation, opinion, description) related to the general topic or theme of the text.

Format:

The question-answer format is usually short answer or extended response (essay).

Directions: Reread the passage on page 3. Answer the questions and identify the QAR. On the next page, write the strategies you used to find the answers.

QUESTION / ANSWER / QAR

1. What did audiences of the antislavery speakers criticize?

   QAR: _____

2. What were some rights women lacked in the 1800s?

   QAR: _____

3. In this passage, the term *abolitionists* refers to what?

   QAR: _____

4. What is our society's attitude toward women's rights today?

   QAR: _____

Concept Lesson 1

STRATEGY

1.

2.

3.

4.

Directions: Write a short-answer question about the text on page 3 for each type of QAR. Then tell why the question represents that QAR.

Right There

Question   **Answer**   **Why this is a Right There QAR**

Think and Search

Question   **Answer**   **Why this is a Think and Search QAR**

Author and Me

Question   **Answer**   **Why this is an Author and Me QAR**

On My Own

Question   **Answer**   **Why this is an On My Own QAR**

Directions: Write four new questions about the text on page 3 in the spaces provided. (Do not fill in the answers.) When instructed to do so, exchange your *Student Activity Book* with a partner and answer each other's questions.

Partner's Name: _____

Directions: Answer each question, identify the QAR, and explain how you know what kind of QAR it is.

1.

   Answer:

   QAR:

   How do you know:

2.

   Answer:

   QAR:

   How do you know:

Concept Lesson 1

3.

   Answer:

   QAR:

   How do you know:

4.

   Answer:

   QAR:

   How do you know:

Directions: Read this passage from *Sue at the Field Museum*.

Sue the T-Rex

The first *T. rex* specimen was found in 1900. Since then, only seven skeletons that are more than half complete have been discovered. Of these, Sue is the largest, most complete, and best preserved *T. rex* ever found. Most of Sue's bones are in excellent condition and have a high degree of surface detail. Sixty-seven million years after her death, it is still possible to see fine details showing where muscles, tendons, and other soft tissues rested against or attached to the bone. Sue's completeness, combined with the exquisite preservation of the bones, makes her an invaluable scientific resource, permitting highly detailed study of *T. rex* anatomy.

In the summer of 1990, Sue Hendrickson was working as a fossil hunter with a commercial fossil-collecting team near Faith, South Dakota. On August 12 most of the team went into town to get a flat tire fixed and to take a short break from the heat. Sue stayed behind to look for fossils. She hiked over to some sandstone bluffs that had previously caught her attention. Within minutes she spotted some bone fragments on the ground. She scanned the cliffs above to find out where the fragments had fallen from and saw dinosaur bones—big ones. She climbed up the cliff for a better look at the bones, and saw they were huge. She thought she had found a *T. rex*, and when the team returned, they confirmed her find and promptly named it "Sue" in her honor.

Soon after Sue was discovered, her bones became the center of a dispute. Who owned the fossil?

To dig up dinosaurs, you always need the landowner's permission. But in Sue's case it was unclear whose land it was because . . . the bones were found on land that was part of a Sioux Indian reservation, BUT . . . the land belonged to a private rancher, BUT . . . the rancher was part Sioux, and his land was held in trust by the U.S. government. While people argued about who owned Sue, the bones were safely locked away in storerooms at the South Dakota School of Mines and Technology. In the end, a judge decided that Sue was held in trust by the U.S. government for the rancher on whose property the skeleton had been found. The rancher, in turn, decided to sell Sue at public auction.

Following the long custody battle, Sue was sold at Sotheby's auction house in New York on October 4, 1997. Just eight minutes after the bidding started, the Field Museum of Chicago purchased Sue for nearly $8.4 million—the most money ever paid for a fossil. On May 17, 2000, the Field Museum unveiled Sue, the largest, most complete, and best preserved *T. rex* fossil yet discovered.

Directions: Answer the questions below about the text on page 11. Then, identify the text structure and the strategy you used to find the answer.

QUESTION / ANSWER

1. Who found Sue?
   A. A rancher
   B. A hike
   C. A professional fossil hunter
   D. None of the above

2. What happened after Sue was found?
   A. The ownership of the bones was contested.
   B. The bones were temporarily stored at a university.
   C. The bones were put on display at a museum.
   D. All of the above.

3. Why was the ownership of the bones unclear?

4. Why was Sue an important find?

12 Concept Lesson 2

TEXT STRUCTURE

1.

2.

3.

4.

STRATEGY

1.

2.

3.

4.

Directions: Write two short-answer Think and Search questions about the text on page 11. Then for each question, write the answer, identify the text structure, and tell why the QAR is Think and Search.

1.

Answer:

Text Structure:

Why this is a Think and Search QAR:

2.

Answer:

Text Structure:

Why this is a Think and Search QAR:

Directions: Write two new questions about the text on page 11 in the spaces provided. (Do not fill in the answers.) When instructed to do so, exchange your *Student Activity Book* with a partner and answer each other's questions.

Partner's Name: _____

Directions: Answer each question, identify the QAR, explain how you know what kind of QAR it is, and identify the strategies you used.

1.

   Answer:

   QAR:

   How do you know:

   Strategies for finding the answer:

2.

   Answer:

   QAR:

   How do you know:

   Strategies for finding the answer:

Concept Lesson 2

In My Head Sample Questions

1. **Author and Me: Text to Self**
   - How would you feel if you were the main character?
   - Compare your experience with that of someone in the story.
   - How does the situation today reflect the outcome of events described in the text?

   Notes:

2. **Author and Me: Text to Text**
   - Compare the main character with a character in another text you have read. How is he or she the same or different?

   Notes:

3. **Author and Me: Text to Themes**
   - What is the theme of the story?
   - What do you think was the author's primary message to the reader?

   Notes:

4. **On My Own**
   - Do you think women have full civil rights? Why or why not? Explain your conclusion.
   - Describe a time when you were scared. Why were you frightened? What happened?

   Notes:

Directions: Read this excerpt from *The Red Badge of Courage: An Episode of the American Civil War* by Stephen Crane. Then answer the questions on the next page.

The Red Badge of Courage

The cold passed reluctantly from the earth, and the retiring fogs revealed an army stretched out on the hills, resting. As the landscape changed from brown to green, the army awakened, and began to tremble with eagerness at the noise of rumors….

Once a certain tall soldier developed virtues and went resolutely to wash a shirt. He came flying back from a brook waving his garment bannerlike. He was swelled with a tale he had heard from a reliable friend, who had heard it from a truthful cavalryman, who had heard it from his trustworthy brother, one of the orderlies at division headquarters. He adopted the important air of a herald in red and gold. "We're goin' t' move t' morrah—sure," he said pompously to a group in the company street. "We're goin' 'way up the river, cut across, an' come around in behint 'em."

To his attentive audience he drew a loud and elaborate plan of a very brilliant campaign. When he had finished, the blue-clothed men scattered into small arguing groups between the rows of squat brown huts…. "It's a lie! that's all it is—a thunderin' lie!" said another private loudly. His smooth face was flushed, and his hands were thrust sulkily into his trousers' pockets. He took the matter as an affront to him. "I don't believe the derned old army's ever going to move. We're set. I've got ready to move eight times in the last two weeks, and we ain't moved yet."

The tall soldier felt called upon to defend the truth of a rumor he himself had introduced. He and the loud one came near to fighting over it….

Many of the men engaged in a spirited debate. One outlined in a peculiarly lucid manner all the plans of the commanding general. He was opposed by men who advocated that there were other plans of campaign. They clamored at each other, numbers making futile bids for the popular attention. Meanwhile, the soldier who had fetched the rumor bustled about with much importance….

There was a youthful private who listened with eager ears to the words of the tall soldier and to the varied comments of his comrades. After receiving a fill of discussions concerning marches and attacks, he went to his hut and crawled through an intricate hole that served it as a door. He wished to be alone with some new thoughts that had lately come to him….

The youth was in a little trance of astonishment. So they were at last going to fight. On the morrow, perhaps, there would be a battle, and he would be in it. For a time he was obliged to labor to make himself believe. He could not accept with assurance an omen that he was about to mingle in one of those great affairs of the earth.

He had, of course, dreamed of battles all his life—of vague and bloody conflicts that had thrilled him with their sweep and fire. In visions he had seen himself in many struggles. He had imagined peoples secure in the shadow of his eagle-eyed prowess. But awake he had regarded battles as crimson blotches on the pages of the past. He had put them as things of the bygone with his thought-images of heavy crowns and high castles. There was a portion of the world's history which he had regarded as the time of wars, but it, he thought, had been long gone over the horizon and had disappeared forever.

Directions: Answer the following questions about the text on page 17. Indicate the type of QAR, where you found the answer, and the strategies you used to find the answer.

QUESTION / ANSWER / QAR

1. Describe how the soldiers responded to the rumor of battle and how you react to rumors or gossip that you hear.

   QAR: _____

2. The "youth" in this passage "was about to mingle in one of those great affairs of the earth." Compare this "great affair" with an event in another story you have read.

   QAR: _____

3. In this passage, one of the author's themes is

   A. how the uncertainty of war affected the soldiers
   B. people will believe anything they hear
   C. the soldiers were not afraid to die
   D. the virtues of bravery

   QAR: _____

4. What would it be like to be a soldier facing battle? What would your thoughts and concerns be?

   QAR: _____

SOURCE	STRATEGY
1.	1.
2.	2.
3.	3.
4.	4.

Directions: Write two short-answer In My Head questions about the text on page 17. Then write the answers and why the QAR categories are In My Head.

Question	Answer	Why this is an In My Head QAR

Question	Answer	Why this is an In My Head QAR

Concept Lesson 3

Directions: Write two new questions about the text on page 17 in the spaces provided. (Do not fill in the answers.) When instructed to do so, exchange your *Student Activity Book* with a partner and answer each other's questions.

Partner's Name: _____

Directions: Answer each question, identify the QAR, and explain how you know what type of QAR it is.

1.

   Answer:

   QAR:

   How do you know:

2.

   Answer:

   QAR:

   How do you know:

Concept Lesson 3

Test-Taking Strategies

Before you read the text…
- Read the test questions first.
- Scan for key words in the text.
- Skim first and last sentences; read the text quickly to find the main idea.

As you read…
- Circle, underline, or highlight key words or phrases.
- Identify important information and make notes.
- Predict what will happen next.
- Connect to the text. Ask yourself: What do I already know about this topic? What else have I read about this topic? Have I experienced something similar?
- Identify the theme.

Before you answer the question…
- Reread the question.
- Identify the QAR.
- Reread or skim the text.
- Scan your notes and words or phrases that you highlighted in the text.
- Brainstorm an answer and briefly note your thoughts. For an essay question, make a short outline of your answer.

For your answer…
- Summarize, infer, draw conclusions, or make connections.
- Support your answer with details from the text.
- Write complete sentences. Use conventional grammar, punctuation, and spelling.
- Pace yourself. Don't spend too much time on any one answer.

Directions: Read the following excerpt from *Ellen Foster* by Kaye Gibbons.

Chapter 1, Part 1

When I was little I would think of ways to kill my daddy…

He drank his own self to death the year after the County moved me out… And I can say for a fact that I am better off now than when he was alive.

I live in a clean brick house and mostly I am left to myself. When I start to carry an odor I take a bath and folks tell me how sweet I look.

There is a plenty to eat here and if we run out of something we just go to the store and get some more. I had me a egg sandwich for breakfast, mayonnaise on both sides. And I may fix me another one for lunch.

Two years ago I did not have much of anything. Not that I live in the lap of luxury now but I am proud for the schoolbus to pick me up here every morning. My stylish well-groomed self standing in the front yard with the grass green and the hedge bushes square.

I figure I made out pretty good considering the rest of my family is either dead or crazy…

Oh but I do remember when I was scared. Everything was so wrong like somebody had knocked something loose and my family was shaking itself to death. Some wild ride broke and the one in charge strolled off and let us spin and shake and fly off the rail. And they both died tired of the wild crazy spinning and wore out and sick…

Even my mama's skin looked tired of holding in her weak self. She would prop herself up by the refrigerator and watch my daddy go round the table swearing at all who did him wrong. She looked all sad in her face like it was all her fault.

She comes home from the hospital sometimes. If I was her I would stay there. All laid up in the air conditioning with folks patting your head and bringing you fruit baskets.

Oh no. She comes in and he lets into her right away. Carrying on. Set up in his E-Z lounger like he is King for a Day. You bring me this or that he might say.

She comes in the door and he asks about supper right off. What does she have planned? he wants to know. Wouldn't he like to know what I myself have planned?… More like a big mean baby than a grown man…

Big wind-up toy of a man. He is just too sorry to talk back to even if he is my daddy. And she is too limp and too sore to get up the breath to push the words out to stop it all. She just stands there and lets him work out his evil on her.

Get in the kitchen and fix me something to eat. I had to cook the whole time you was gone, he tells her.

And that was some lie he made up. Cook for his own self. Ha. If I did not feed us both we had to go into town and get take-out chicken. I myself was looking forward to something fit to eat but I was not about to say anything.

Directions: Complete this chart as you work together with your peers and teacher.

QUESTION / ANSWER / QAR

1. The relationship Ellen had with her dad was that
    A. he took care of her
    B. she took care of him
    C. she lived away from him
    D. she admired him

    QAR: _____

2. What has happened to Ellen in the past two years?

    QAR: _____

3. Compare Ellen's old life with her new life.

    QAR: _____

4. What does Ellen value most in life?

    QAR: _____

STRATEGY

1.

2.

3.

4.

Directions: Read more from *Ellen Foster*. Then answer the questions on pages 27 through 29.

Chapter 1, Part 2

Nobody yells after anybody to do this or that here.

My new mama lays out the food and we all take a turn to dish it out. Then we eat and have a good time. Toast or biscuits with anything you please. Eggs any style. Corn cut off the cob the same day we eat it. I keep my elbows off the table and wipe my mouth like a lady. …When everybody is done eating my new mama puts the dishes in a thing, shuts the door, cuts on it, and Wa-La they are clean

My mama does not say a word about being tired or sore. She did ask who kept everything so clean and he took the credit. I do not know who he thinks he fooled. I knew he lied and my mama did too. She just asked to be saying something.

Mama puts the food out on the table and he wants to know what I am staring at. At you humped over your plate like one of us is about to snatch it from you. You old hog. But I do not say it.

Why don't you eat? he wants to know.

I don't have an appetite, I say back.

Well, you better eat. Your mama looks like this might be her last supper.

He is so sure he's funny that he laughs at his own self…

Now at my new mama's I lay up late in the day and watch the rain fall outside. Not one thing is pressing on me to get done here.

I have a bag of candy to eat on. One piece at a time. Make it last. All I got left to do is eat supper and wash myself.

Look around my room. It is so nice.

When I accumulate enough money I plan to get some colored glass things that you dangle from the window glass. I lay here and feature how that would look. I already got pink checkerboard curtains with dingleballs around the edges. My new mama sewed them for me. She also sewed matching sacks that I cram my pillows into every morning.

Everything matches. It is all so neat and clean…

The yelling makes my mama jump and if she was asleep she is awake now. Grits her teeth every time he calls out damn this or that. The more he drinks the less sense he makes.

By the time the dog races come on he's stretched out on the bathroom floor and can't get up. I know I need to go in there and poke him. Same thing every Saturday…

I get up and go in there and tell him to get up that folks got to come in here and do their business.

He can go lay in the truck.

He just grunts and grabs at my ankle and misses.

Get on up I say again to him. You got to be firm when he is like this. He'd lay there and rot if I let him so I nudge him with my foot. I will not touch my hands to him. Makes me want to heave my own self seeing him pull himself up on the sink. He zig-zags out through the living room and

Chapter 1, Part 2 (continued)

I guess he makes it out the door. I don't hear him fall down the steps.

And where did she come from? Standing in the door looking at it all.

Get back in bed, I say to mama.

Mama's easy to tend to. She goes back in the bedroom. Not a bit of trouble. Just stiff and hard to move around. I get her back in the bed and tell her he's outside for the night. She starts to whimper and I say it is no reason to cry. But she will wear herself out crying.

I ought to lock him out.

A grown man that should be bringing her food to nibble on and books to look at. No but he is taking care of his own self tonight. Just like she is not sick or kin to him.

A storm is coming up. And I will lay here with my mama until I see her chest rise up and sink down regular. Deep and regular and far away from the man in the truck.

Directions: Answer the questions below and on the next two pages. Identify the QAR categories and the test-taking strategies you used.

1. Ellen is most upset that her father
   A. doesn't work
   B. abuses her mother
   C. does not take care of her mother
   D. does not take care of her

   QAR: _____

   Test-Taking Strategy:

2. Describe Ellen's feelings toward her father during the scene when her mother has returned home.

   QAR: _____
   Test-Taking Strategy:

Concept Lesson 4

3. What role has Ellen taken on in her birth family and why?

   QAR: _____

   Test-Taking Strategy:

4. Ellen's feelings toward her father could best be described as
   A. anger
   B. pity
   C. disgust
   D. A and B
   E. A and C

   QAR: _____

   Test-Taking Strategy:

5. Describe the stability and simple pleasures of Ellen's new life.

   QAR: _____

   Test-Taking Strategy:

6. If Ellen went to your school, what would you think of her? Give specific examples and reasons.

   QAR: _____

   Test-Taking Strategy:

7. Ellen's new life is like her old one because
   A. no one yells
   B. her mother takes care of her
   C. she has plenty to eat
   D. she lives in a messy place
   E. none of the above

   QAR: _____

   Test-Taking Strategy:

8. How does Ellen's birth mother react to her husband?

   QAR: _____

   Test-Taking Strategy:

9. Compare and contrast Ellen's new life with her old life. Use details from the story to support your answer.

   QAR: _____

   Test-Taking Strategy:

10. Ellen had to struggle to survive in her birth family. Describe a personal experience in which you struggled for success, happiness, stability, approval, or some other goal.

    QAR: _____

    Test-Taking Strategy:

Directions: Read the following article by Marcella J. Kehus.

The Complexities of Cloning

Before 1996, few people had actually considered cloning a real possibility beyond something you might read about or see in a science fiction movie. But in July of that year, when Dolly the ewe (baby sheep) was born as a clone of her mother, some great debates began that are still raging in many areas. Cloning, or the creating of a living replica from DNA from a body cell, took quite a long time to develop before it actually worked with Dolly as its first success. Now people from politicians to religious leaders to scientists and the general public continue to argue over whether this technology should be applied to humans. The basic debate comes down to: Should we or should we not allow the cloning of human beings? And, if we do so, what are the possible results?

Now that the procedure for cloning has been discovered, it seems only a matter of time before it is applied to humans. This is where a number of people, specialists and general citizens alike, have serious concerns. One of their primary concerns, which often comes up with every new technology, are the number of ways that such a technology might be abused. For example, what if a certain group wanted to use cloning to create an army of exact duplicate soldiers or creatures to carry out their evil deeds? And, because cloning can include genetic engineering, or selecting just the right genes to create a certain kind of being (strong, green eyes, etc.), the idea of creating a look-alike super-human race reminds people quickly of the terrible possibilities of Hitler-like beliefs if given the power of cloning.

There are lesser kinds of abuses that the power of human cloning could inspire. Perhaps a former football player got his career cut short due to an injury; what would keep him from creating a clone of himself to play and become the star he always wanted to be? Cloning could become a fashionable way for other conceited people to just re-create themselves and the result may be a child who is never given a chance to become an individual.

On the other hand, there are impressive possibilities when it comes to human cloning. First, cloning is another possible solution for couples who are otherwise unable to have children of their own. In fact, the medical solutions made possible by clones are numerous including the supplying of life-saving transplant organs or bone marrow by cloned family members that would automatically match. And, when coupled with genetic engineering, cloning may allow us to create better humans as we discover more and more about disease and aging and produce clones who are better-equipped to survive.

Certainly, the possibilities of human cloning are scientifically possible. Yet, as with other new developments, one must carefully consider the possible outcomes—both good and bad. Ultimately, we as a society will make the decision as to whether human cloning's benefits outweigh its possible abuses and where we go from here.

Directions: Answer the following questions about the article on page 30 and identify each QAR.

1. According to the article, what "great debate" started in 1996?

   QAR: _____

2. What are other arguments against cloning that are not mentioned in the article?

   QAR: _____

3. Who is involved in the debate about human cloning?

   QAR: _____

4. What do you think is the strongest reason given for human cloning? Why?

   QAR: _____

Concept Lesson 5

5. What do you think is the strongest reason against human cloning? Why?

   QAR: _____

6. What are three different ways that individuals might benefit from human cloning?

   QAR: _____

7. Who do you think will make the final decision about whether or not human cloning is allowed?

   QAR: _____

Essay-Writing Tips, Part 1

- Before you start writing, identify the QAR.

- Create a short outline of your main thesis or idea and two or three main points that support your thesis. If you're stuck, do some brainstorming.

- Restate the question as a thesis or opening line(s).

- Answer all parts of the question. Check off each part as you go.

- For each part of the answer, note the specific part in the text that supports it.

- Include an introduction, at least two body paragraphs, and a conclusion.

- Present your ideas in a logical way. What comes first, second, third? What is your conclusion?

- If you have time, reread your essay to correct spelling, punctuation, or grammatical errors.

Directions: Reread the passage on page 30. Then choose a side for or against human cloning and write an essay to convince your audience to believe as you do.

Directions: Read "The Bungee Lunge" on pages 36 and 37. As you read, write five during reading questions in the spaces below. Identify the QAR that each question represents.

1.

   QAR: _____

2.

   QAR: _____

3.

   QAR: _____

4.

   QAR: _____

5.

   QAR: _____

Booster Lesson 1

Directions: Read this article by Karen McNulty.

The Bungee Lunge

Here's your giant rubber band. Now jump! It's only a 10-story plunge—and science will spring you back.

The Science Behind the Bounce

Ready?

When standing high on a jump platform, you have lots of potential (stored) energy.

Jump!

Leap off and your potential energy is converted to kinetic energy, the energy of motion. For a few seconds, you experience free fall, until there's no more slack in the cord.

Stret – t – ch

Then the cord starts to stretch. This stores the energy of your fall in the cord.

Bounce

This stored energy springs you back up. You fall and bounce again… and again…

Phew!

Each bounce disperses some of your energy, so eventually you stop. You'll have to hang around until someone lowers you to a raft or the ground.

You're hanging onto the railing of a bridge, 46 m above the river. Your friends on the bank below seem awfully small; looking at them makes you dizzy. Someone standing behind you is counting down "Three…two…one!" Defying every sane notion in your brain, you leap—headfirst.

The 100 km/h fall toward the water terrifies you. But just as you close your eyes for the icy plunge, something happens: You bounce back!

Better thank your lucky *bungee cord*—that wrist-thick band of latex rubber strapped to your ankles and anchored to the bridge. Because it was the right length, it kept you high and dry. And because it stret-t-t-ched and recoiled—giving you a few good bounces—it used up the energy of your fall so you didn't get torn limb from limb. Phew!

Those who have done it say it's the thrill of a lifetime—"a natural high." Others call it crazy. But everyone knows it as "bungee jumping," the sport springing up (and down) across the nation.

At least one group of people has been "bungee jumping" for ages: the men of Pentecost Island in the South Pacific. They make cords from elastic vines, lash them to their ankles, and plunge off wooden towers into pits of softened earth. For these islanders, jumping is a springtime ritual, meant to demonstrate courage and supposedly ensure a plentiful yam harvest.

In North America, jumpers take the bungee plunge just for the excitement of it. Scott Bergman, who runs a bungee-jumping company in California, explains the appeal. "It's a feeling of having absolutely no control—and loving it."

And it doesn't take any skill. Just $75 to $100 and *faith*—in physics. It's a simple physics equation, after all, that let's "jump masters" like Bergman determine how far the cord will stretch when you take the plunge—whether it will stretch too far.

The Bungee Lunge (continued)

Weighing the Odds

The major variables are the stretchiness, or *elasticity*, of the cord—predetermined by the manufacturer—and the jumper's weight. As you might guess, "the heavier you are, the more the cord is going to stretch," says physicist Peter Brancazio.

By weighing customers (they don't just ask), using the equation, and adjusting cords, jump masters have bounced thousands to safety. (There have been some deaths—usually caused by frayed cords or other faulty equipment.)

Jump experts can even adjust the cords to give their clients custom-made thrills. "When we jump off bridges in California," says Bergman, "we ask the people if they want to just touch the water, dunk their heads in, or go all the way. We can really get it that exact."

Really? "I wouldn't trust them," says Brancazio, "but I guess they can."

If, for example, Bergman calculates that you'll crack your skull on a rock in the river, he can shorten your cord. "That starts the stretch at a higher point off the ground," says Brancazio.

Or you can jump with two cords. "In that case," says Brancazio, your weight is "equally divided between the cords so each stretches half as far."

Chances are, you'll scream just as hard with fear and delight.

Directions: Write a short answer to the following questions based on the article on pages 36 and 37 and identify the QAR for each.

1. Explain how energy is stored and released in a bungee cord.

   QAR: _____

2. Summarize the points of view of the two experts (Scott Bergman and Peter Brancazio) quoted in the article. Why might they have different perspectives on bungee jumping?

   QAR: _____

3. Would you ever consider bungee jumping? What would be your major considerations in making a decision?

   QAR: _____

4. Compare bungee jumping in the South Pacific to California.

   QAR: _____

5. Compare the during reading questions you wrote on page 35 with the questions above. What types of QAR categories are there? Which of your questions prepared you for the questions asked above, if any?

   QAR: _____

Booster Lesson 1

Tips for Using Textbooks

Look at text features:

- Headings and subheadings
- Summaries (main idea, key points)
- Terms and their definitions
- Words bolded or highlighted in the text
- Captions for illustrations

Use previewing techniques:

- Preview comprehension questions or exercises at the end.
- Skim the first and last sentences of each paragraph.

Take notes and ask questions:

- Restate definitions and explanations in your own words.
- Connect to the text: What do I already know? What do I want to learn?
- Restate or paraphrase questions in your own words.

Directions: Read this passage from *American History: The Early Years to 1877*.

The Women's Rights Movement

Guide to Reading

Main Idea
Emboldened by their work in the antislavery movement, many women fought to improve their own status in society.

Read to Learn...
* why women became unhappy with their positions in the mid-1800s
* how working in the antislavery movement prepared women to fight for their own rights
* what arguments opponents used against the women's rights movement

Terms to Know
* abolitionist
* suffrage

Women took a special interest in the antislavery movement. As they fought for social reform for African Americans, they realized that they also lacked full social and political rights. When women such as Angelina and Sarah Grimké tried to participate actively in the antislavery movement, they often met resistance. As a result, many abolitionists became crusaders for women's rights.

Equal rights for women would require major reform. In the 1800s women actually had fewer rights than in colonial times. They had few political or legal rights. Women could not vote. They could not hold public office. A woman's husband owned all her property.

Antislavery Movement Gives Women a Boost

Women from New England to Ohio joined the antislavery societies. They worked hard, gathering signatures on thousands of petitions to send to Congress. They also read about and discussed the abuses of slavery. Many saw similarities between the treatment of enslaved persons and women.

In her book *Woman in the Nineteenth Century,* journalist **Margaret Fuller** observed that "there exists in the minds of men a tone of feeling toward women as towards slaves." Abolitionists Angelina and Sarah Grimké confronted this feeling when they spoke to antislavery groups. Audiences did not criticize their stand on slavery. They did, though, question their right to speak in public.

As a result, the Grimkés soon found themselves in the midst of "an entirely new contest—a contest for the rights of woman." Sarah wrote that "all I ask... is that [men] will take their feet from off our necks and permit us to stand upright."

The Women's Rights Movement

Their involvement in the antislavery movement and other reform movements gave women roles outside their homes and families. They learned valuable skills, such as organizing, working

The Women's Rights Movement (continued)

together, and speaking in public. Eventually they used these skills to further their own cause—the women's rights movement.

In 1840 nine women from the United States attended the World Anti-Slavery Convention in **London.** When the women arrived at the convention, however, the male delegates barred them from participating. The women and some male allies protested. On the first day of the convention, delegates debated the situation.

Clergy at the convention considered it improper for women to participate. Other male delegates declared women "unfit for public or business meetings." In the end, the majority of delegates decided that women could not take part in discussions. Instead, the women delegates would have to sit in the gallery behind a curtain.

Humiliated and angry, two of the women, Lucretia Coffin Mott and Elizabeth Cady Stanton, spent hours after the meetings talking about women's position in society. They realized that they could not bring about social change if they themselves lacked social and political rights. Stanton and Mott "resolved to hold a convention as soon as we returned home, and form a society to advocate the rights of women."

The Seneca Falls Convention

Eight years passed before the two friends organized their convention. On July 19, 1848, the first women's rights convention opened in Seneca Falls, New York. Both male and female delegates attended the convention. The delegates issued the Seneca Falls Declaration, which proclaimed that "all men and women are created equal."

Then the declaration listed several resolutions. One of them demanded suffrage, or the right to vote, for women. Even supporters of women's rights hesitated to pass this bold demand. Mott exclaimed, "Oh, Lizzie, thou will make us ridiculous! We must go slowly." But Stanton refused to withdraw the resolution. After much heated debate, it passed by a narrow margin.

The Seneca Falls Convention marked the beginning of an organized women's rights movement. Following the convention, women did not achieve all of their demands. They did, however, overcome some obstacles. Many states passed laws permitting women to own their own property and keep their earnings. Many men and women, though, continued to oppose the movement. Most politicians ignored or acted hostile to the issue of women's rights.

The Women's Rights Movement (continued)

Assessment

Check for Understanding
1. Define suffrage.
2. Why did women become unhappy with their position in the mid-1800s? About what areas of their daily lives were they most concerned?

Critical Thinking
3. **Comparing and Contrasting.** Contrast the views of the men and women who opposed the women's rights movement with those who supported it.

4. **Identifying Relationships.** Re-create the diagram shown here, and list how women's work in the antislavery movement prepared them to fight for their own rights.

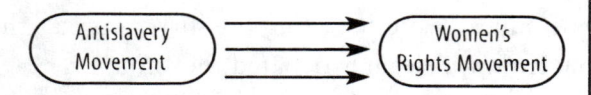

Antislavery Movement → Women's Rights Movement

Interdisciplinary Activity

5. **Citizenship.** Are women today denied any rights that men have? Draw up an agenda for a new Seneca Falls Convention listing topics for discussion.

Booster Lesson 2

Directions: Read "The Women's Rights Movement" on pages 40 and 41 and answer the questions from the Assessment section on page 42. Identify the type of QAR each question represents.

1.

   QAR: _____

2.

   QAR: _____

3.

   QAR: _____

4.

   QAR: _____

5.

   Write your agenda on a separate sheet or in your "QAR Reflections Journal."

   QAR: _____

Directions: Read this letter to President Franklin D. Roosevelt.

Dear Mr. President

Phila., Pa.
November 26, 1934

Honorable Franklin D. Roosevelt
Washington, D.C.

Dear Mr. President:

I am forced to write to you because we find ourselves in a very serious condition. For the last three or four years we have had depression and suffered with my family and little children severely. Now Since the Home Owners Loan Corporation opened up, I have been going up there in order to save my home, because there has been unemployment in my house for more than three years. You can imagine that I and my family have suffered from lack of water supply in my house for more than two years. Last winter I did not have coal and the pipes burst in my house and therefore could not make heat in the house. Now winter is here again and we are suffering of cold, no water in the house, and we are facing to be forced out of the house, because I have no money to move or pay so much money as they want when after making settlement. I am mother of little children, am sick and losing my health, and we are eight people in the family, and where can I go when I don't have money because no one is working in my house. The Home Loan Corporation wants $42. a month rent or else we will have to be on the street. I am living in this house for about ten years and when times were good we would put our last cent in the house and now I have no money, no home and no wheres to go. I beg of you to please help me and my family and little children for the sake of a sick mother and a suffering family to give this your immediate attention so we will not be forced to move or put out in the street.

Waiting and Hoping that you will act quickly.
Thanking you very much I remain

Mrs. E. L.

Directions: Read this excerpt from a speech by Robert Kennedy.

On the Death of Dr. Martin Luther King

This speech was given by Robert F. Kennedy on April 4, 1968, shortly after Dr. Martin Luther King, Jr. had been assassinated. At the time, Robert Kennedy was a U.S. Senator leading a race for the presidency, but he was assassinated a few months later.

Martin Luther King dedicated his life to love and to justice between fellow human beings. He died in the cause of that effort. In this difficult day, in this difficult time for the United States, it's perhaps well to ask what kind of a nation we are and what direction we want to move in.

For those of you who are black—considering the evidence evidently is that there were white people who were responsible—you can be filled with bitterness, and with hatred, and a desire for revenge.

We can move in that direction as a country, in greater polarization—black people amongst blacks, and white amongst whites, filled with hatred toward one another. Or we can make an effort, as Martin Luther King did, to understand and to comprehend, and replace that violence, that stain of bloodshed that has spread across our land, with an effort to understand, compassion and love.

For those of you who are black and are tempted to be filled with hatred and mistrust of the injustice of such an act, against all white people, I would only say that I can also feel in my own heart the same kind of feeling. I had a member of my family killed, but he was killed by a white man.

But we have to make an effort in the United States, we have to make an effort to understand, to get beyond these rather difficult times.

My favorite poet was Aeschylus. He once wrote: "Even in our sleep, pain which cannot forget falls drop by drop upon the heart, until, in our own despair, against our will, comes wisdom through the awful grace of God."

What we need in the United States is not division; what we need in the United States is not hatred; what we need in the United States is not violence and lawlessness, but is love and wisdom, and compassion toward one another, and a feeling of justice toward those who still suffer within our country, whether they be white or whether they be black.

So I ask you tonight to return home, to say a prayer for the family of Martin Luther King, yeah that's true, but more importantly to say a prayer for our own country, which all of us love—a prayer for understanding and that compassion of which I spoke. We can do well in this country. We will have difficult times. We've had difficult times in the past. And we will have difficult times in the future. It is not the end of violence; it is not the end of lawlessness; and it's not the end of disorder.

But the vast majority of white people and the vast majority of black people in this country want to live together, want to improve the quality of our life, and want justice for all human beings that abide in our land.

Let us dedicate ourselves to what the Greeks wrote so many years ago: to tame the savageness of man and make gentle the life of this world.

Let us dedicate ourselves to that, and say a prayer for our country and for our people.

Directions: Read pages 44 and 45 and then answer the following questions. Identify the QAR after your answer.

1. Compare and contrast the audience, purpose, and writing style of the two passages.

   QAR: _____

2. If you were President Roosevelt, how would you have responded to Mrs. E. L.'s letter? Why?

   QAR: _____

3. What would have been your reaction to Robert F. Kennedy's speech at the time. Why?

   QAR: _____

Best-Answer Strategies

IN THE BOOK

Right There
- Reread.
- Scan for key words.
- Recall key facts or figures.

Think and Search
- Reread.
- Scan for key words.
- Skim first and last sentences.
- Identify important information.
- Look for specific examples.
- Identify characters or people, events, plot, problem and solutions, etc.
- Identify the main idea or theme.
- Predict what will happen next.

IN MY HEAD

Author and Me
- Reread.
- Skim first and last sentences.
- Connect to important information What do I already know about this subject?
- Connect to the characters or people and events in the text.
- Connect to the main idea or theme.
- Predict what will happen next.
- Connect to other texts. What have I read before on this same subject or with this same theme?

On My Own
- Reread.
- Connect to the general theme or topic.
- Connect to other texts. What have I read before on this same subject or with this same theme?

Booster Lesson 4

Directions: Read this passage from *Lasers* by Lynne Kelly and answer the questions on page 49.

How a Laser Beam Is Made

The first pulse laser was made by Theodore H. Maiman of the United States in 1960. He used a ruby rod to make a short flash of laser light. The method has been improved since then, but the idea is the same.

1. A rod of ruby, about the size of a finger is used. Real ruby is very expensive, but synthetic ruby can be used.

2. The ends of the ruby rod are ground so they are perfectly smooth and parallel to each other. Each end is painted silver to make mirrors, but one end receives a thinner layer of paint than the other. This means that this end is only partially reflective.

3. A flash tube is wrapped around the ruby rob and connected to a battery. The flash tube and battery act as the power source.

4. When the flash tube is switched on, it produces bright, white light. This excites, or increases, the energy level of chromium atoms in the ruby. Light is reflected back and forth along the rod.

5. After a fraction of a second, a bright flash of red laser light will come out of the end of the ruby rod.

When the flash tube is switched on, chromium atoms in the ruby rod absorb some of the light energy. These atoms then give out energy again in the form of colored light. Light beams given out from one sort of atom that has been excited in this way will all be identical.

These identical light beams reflect back and forth along the ruby rod from one mirror to the other. As they do so, they excite more atoms, which give off more light. This goes on until the light beam has grown strong enough to break through the thinner mirror. All the light beams emitted from the thinner mirror will be identical and coherent and will travel in a straight line. They will be a laser beam.

The name *laser* comes from the way in which a laser beam is made. It is a form of light that is the result of many reflections between the mirrors on the ends of the ruby rod. This causes the energy to increase, or amplify. The chromium atoms that give off the pure light beam have been excited, or stimulated, by the flash of light. The atoms give out, or emit, pure monochromatic light, which is a form of electromagnetic radiation.

So a laser beam is the result of Light Amplification by Stimulated Emission of Radiation.

Directions: Answer the following questions about the text on page 48.

1. Which list includes the items used in generating laser light?
   A. ruby rod, flash tube, light switch
   B. synthetic ruby, mirrors, chromium atoms
   C. ruby rod, flash tube, battery
   D. ruby rod, reflective coating, flash tube, battery

2. What is the purpose of the mirrors at each end of the rod?
   A. They intensify the energy of the light beams as the light beams reflect back and forth between the mirrors.
   B. The protect the ends of the ruby rod as the high energy light beams travel back and forth.
   C. They decrease the level of energy of the chromium atoms in the ruby.
   D. None of the above.

3. What is the purpose of the flash tube and battery?
   A. They hold the ruby rod in place.
   B. They excite the chromium atoms.
   C. They make the light beams coherent.
   D. They generate the power needed to produce the energy for the laser beam.

4. How is a laser beam made?

5. Choose question 1, 2, or 3 above and analyze each response (A, B, C, D). Is it correct, partially correct, or incorrect? Why? Identify a statement or section of the passage that supports your answer.

Booster Lesson 4

The Road Not Taken

Two roads diverged in a yellow wood,
And sorry I could not travel both
And be one traveler, long I stood
And looked down one as far as I could
To where it bent in the undergrowth;

Then took the other, as just as fair,
And having perhaps the better claim,
Because it was grassy and wanted wear;
Though as for that the passing there
Had worn them really about the same,

And both that morning equally lay
In leaves no step had trodden black.
Oh, I kept the first for another day!
Yet knowing how way leads on to way,
I doubted if I should ever come back.

I shall be telling this with a sigh
Somewhere ages and ages hence:
Two roads diverged in a wood, and I—
I took the one less traveled by,
And that has made all the difference.

by Robert Frost

Life

They told me that Life could be just what I made it—
    Life could be fashioned and worn like a gown;
I, the designer; mine the decision
    Whether to wear it with bonnet or crown.

And so I selected the prettiest pattern—
    Life should be made of the rosiest hue—
Something unique, and a bit out of fashion,
    One that perhaps would be chosen by few.

But other folks came and they leaned o'er my shoulder;
    Somebody questioned the ultimate cost;
Somebody tangled the thread I was using;
    One day I found that my scissors were lost.

And somebody claimed the material faded;
    Somebody said I'd be tired ere 'twas worn;
Somebody's fingers, too pointed and spiteful,
    Snatched at the cloth, and I saw it was torn.

Oh! somebody tried to do all the sewing,
    Wanting always to advise or condone.
Here is my life, the product of many;
    Where is that gown I could fashion—alone?

by Nan Terrell Reed

Directions: This test has two parts. When you're finished with Part 1, go on to Part 2.

Part 1

Directions: Read the poems on page 50 and 51. Then write five Author and Me questions (connecting self to text, text to text, and text to theme) about the poems.

Author and Me Questions
for "The Road Not Taken"

1.

2.

3.

4.

5.

Author and Me Questions
for "Life"

1.

2.

3.

4.

5.

Part 2

Directions: Answer the following questions about the two poems. Support your answers with details from the text. Identify the QAR after each answer.

1. In "The Road Not Taken," how did the narrator know that one of the roads was "less traveled by"?

    QAR: _____

2. Why did the narrator choose "the road less traveled by"?

    QAR: _____

3. How does the narrator feel about his decision?

    QAR: _____

Booster Lesson 5

Part 2, continued

4. What is the main idea or theme of "The Road Not Taken"?

   QAR: _____

5. In the poem "Life," what does the author compare life to? What did she want her life to be like?

   QAR: _____

6. Who is the "Somebody" referred to in the poem? What does this somebody do?

   QAR: _____

7. At the end of "Life," how does the narrator feel about her life?

   QAR: _____

Part 2, continued

8. What is the main idea or theme of "Life"?

   QAR: _____

9. Compare and contrast the narrators of the poems "The Road Not Taken" and "Life." What were they seeking? How did they feel about their "road taken" and "gown" at the end?

   QAR: _____

10. Compare and contrast the main ideas or themes in each poem. How are they different? How are they similar?

    QAR: _____

Solving Math Story Problems

Ask yourself...

1. **What is given?**

   Identify the information already stated or given in the problem.

2. **What am I supposed to figure out?**

   Restate the problem in terms of the unknown quantity.

3. **What is the math concept?**

   Identify the math concept or concepts you have to know. What have you already learned about this concept?

Do the work...

4. **Set up the problem.**

5. **Do the calculation.**

6. **Select or write your answer.**

> Always show your work. If you get an incorrect answer because of a computation error, you may get partial credit for setting up the problem correctly and showing how you got the answer.

Booster Lesson 6

Directions: Answer the following question. Refer to the steps on page 56 if necessary.

In Malia's eighth-grade class, 3 out of 5 students are girls. In a class of 30 students, how many are girls?

A. 12
B. 18
C. 20
D. 22

1. What is given?

2. What am I supposed to figure out?

3. What is the math concept?

4. Set up the problem.

5. Do the calculation.

6. Select or write your answer.

Booster Lesson 6

Essay-Writing Tips, Part 2

Purpose

Identify the purpose of the essay:

- Narration
- Information
- Persuasion

Audience

Identify who you are writing for.

Text Type

Identify the text type:

- Formal essay
- Letter
- Editorial
- Newspaper or journal article
- Procedure
- Others

Evaluation

- **Development:** Are the ideas well developed? Does the essay have good supporting or descriptive details?
- **Organization:** Is the essay well organized? Does it have good transitions between ideas and paragraphs?
- **Use of language:** Is the sentence structure varied? Is descriptive or figurative language used effectively?
- **Mechanics:** Do grammatical, spelling, and punctuation errors interfere with understanding the content?

Directions: Complete this worksheet as you work together with your peers and teacher.

ESSAY-WRITING WORKSHEET

Write an article for the school newspaper explaining the benefits of playing computer games.

QAR:

Purpose:

Audience:

Text Type:

Brainstorm Ideas:

Outline:

Directions: With a partner, complete the worksheet. Then write your letter on the next page.

ESSAY-WRITING WORKSHEET

Think of a social issue affecting your school, neighborhood, or community (for example, pollution, noise, litter, homelessness, traffic, etc.). Write a letter to a public official describing the problem and asking for help. Explain what you think should be done to solve it and why.

QAR:

Purpose:

Audience:

Text Type:

Brainstorm Ideas:

Outline:

Directions: Use this page to write your letter.

Booster Lesson 7

Directions: Complete this worksheet and write your essay on the next page.

ESSAY-WRITING WORKSHEET

Imagine that you just saw on the news that computer scientists have perfected the technologies behind artificial intelligence and expect manufacturers to begin making robots soon with many—but not all—human capabilities.

Explain what you and your family members would like robots to do if you could buy them. What kinds of things do you think the robots should or should not do?

QAR:

Purpose:

Audience:

Text Type:

Brainstorm Ideas:

Outline:

Directions: Use this page to write your essay.

Directions: Read the following article from *Teen Vogue*, as told to Sarah Brown by Bess Judson. Then answer the questions on pages 66 through 69.

Survivor

I noticed the bump during the summer. I thought it was cool the way it moved when I swallowed, like a seed sliding under the skin of an orange slice. I made my mom touch it. "Maybe it's a tumor!" I said, laughing. "It's probably just a swollen gland or something. We'll get it checked out if it doesn't go away soon," she said, and sent me off to school.

I was psyched to go to college... My first semester at Hamilton, in upstate New York, was so much fun. I joined the rugby team and started feeling really good about myself again.

I didn't even think about my bump until Christmas break, when I switched from a pediatrician to a general practitioner, who gave me a complete physical. As soon as she felt the lump on my thyroid she sent me for a needle biopsy. I thought it was routine, although I was surprised I went for tests right away, instead of having to schedule an appointment.

And then I went back to school. The first night I was back, my doctor called. The tumor was malignant. I had cancer, and in one week, I was scheduled to have an operation to remove my thyroid. I hung up the phone thinking back to the pink fluid the doctor had removed from my bump during the biopsy. The liquid had looked so harmless inside the syringe, like water used to clean a red paintbrush.

I was totally petrified. As soon as you hear that word—*cancer*—no one knows what to say. Doctors don't really even know that much about it. All they can do is try to cut it out.

My surgeon told me I'd need to take two weeks off from school, which is what I'd planned to do. I spent two nights in the hospital, in and out of sleep. Every few hours a man who called himself the Vampire would wake me up to draw my blood. When I finally stood up to walk, I had to hold my mother's arm to stay on my feet. I inched through the halls, rolling my IV beside me like a fish dragging the rod that hooked it....

Your thyroid is a gland in your neck—the part of your body that regulates metabolism (the physical and chemical processes that essentially maintain life). It also controls a lot of your hormones, and for about a month, I was just miserable. After surgery, I had to wait awhile before I could start taking thyroid-replacement hormones (which simulate the way an actual thyroid works), so my entire hormonal makeup was out of whack. I was tired and I was sad and I would cry all the time about nothing. I was what they call hypothyroid—I felt sluggish and just really crummy.

When I was finally allowed to start taking Synthroid (synthetic thyroid hormones), I was expecting to feel normal right away—to go back to classes and to play rugby in the spring. They have to raise the hormones to the right levels incrementally, so in the beginning, I was taking only about half the level I am now. I went back to school, and I did play rugby, but let's just say I wasn't a huge success. I was so much slower than I'd been before. My friends were totally supportive—they couldn't believe I was playing at all. I signed up for a full course load, but I ended up having to drop a class. In the fall semester, I'd gotten some C's and a D... but this time, somehow, I got straight A's. I think I was just happy to be back, happy I was able to pull through and rebound...

Survivor (continued)

I spent the spring and summer of my junior year studying in Spain. Seeing a different side of life—a side I'd never been exposed to before—gave me a new sense of perspective and taught me not to take so much for granted. When I got back, I knew I wanted to keep learning Spanish—to become fluent to the level of a native speaker, and to do something to help people along the way, if I could.... I had always thought about joining the Peace Corps, but I was never sure I could actually do it...

By my senior year, the more I thought about all the things I'd done, the more I knew that this time, I was strong enough to handle an experience like the Peace Corps. The hardest parts of my life have made me feel the most whole and the proudest of myself. I guess I needed to beat cancer to find out that I can do anything.

Directions: Answer the following questions about the article "Survivor."

1. The subject of "Survivor" was diagnosed with
   A. cancer of the blood (leukemia)
   B. cancer of the thyroid
   C. cancer of the throat
   D. hyperthyroidism
   E. none of the above

2. The thyroid works to regulate your metabolism or
   A. speed of body processes
   B. growth over a lifetime
   C. organ functions
   D. fighting off of disease
   E. none of the above

3. A *biopsy* is
   A. a gland in your neck
   B. a complete physical exam
   C. a procedure to extract blood or tissue from the body for analysis
   D. a drug that regulates your hormones
   E. a needle

4. Some of the symptoms of hypothyroidism are
   A. low energy
   B. depression or sadness
   C. sleeplessness
   D. A and B
   E. A and C

5. Thyroid replacement hormones
    A. cause hormonal imbalance
    B. are called Synthroid
    C. make you feel tired
    D. are effective right away
    E. simulate the way the thyroid works

6. Describe the events in Bess's life leading up to her decision to go into the Peace Corps.

7. Describe how Bess's battle with cancer affected her physically and emotionally. How was her academic and social life affected?

8. How did Bess feel about her experience with cancer?

9. Write an essay describing an experience in which you, someone you know, or a person or character you have read about was a "survivor." What was the experience? How did you or that person or character handle the experience? What were its impacts? What did the experience teach you (or the person or character)?

10. The Peace Corps is a government agency that sends volunteers to developing countries to assist communities in setting up businesses, to teach English, to train health care workers, to plant trees, and to do many other activities depending on the needs of the host country.

Write a letter of application to join the Peace Corps as if you were Bess Judson of "Survivor." Describe why you are a good candidate and the reasons they should accept your application.

QAR Reflections Journal

_____
_____
_____
_____
_____

QAR Reflections Journal

Directions: Read this passage from *American History: The Early Years to 1877* by Donald A. Ritchie and Albert S. Broussard.

The Women's Rights Movement

Women took a special interest in the antislavery movement. As they fought for social reform for African Americans, they realized that they also lacked full social and political rights. When women tried to participate in the antislavery movement, they often met resistance. As a result, many abolitionists became crusaders for women's rights.

Equal rights for women would require major reform. In the 1800s women actually had fewer rights than in colonial times. They had few political or legal rights. Women could not vote or hold public office. A woman's husband owned all of her property.

Women from New England to Ohio joined the antislavery societies. Many saw similarities between the treatment of enslaved persons and women.

Journalist Margaret Fuller observed that "there exists in the minds of men a tone of feeling toward women as towards slaves." Abolitionists Angelina and Sarah Grimké confronted this feeling when they spoke to antislavery groups. Audiences did not criticize their stand on slavery. They did, though, question their right to speak in public.

As a result, the Grimkés soon found themselves in the midst of "an entirely new contest—a contest for the rights of woman." Sarah wrote that "all I ask... is that [men] will take their feet from off our necks and permit us to stand upright."

QAR Characteristics

IN THE BOOK

Right There

Source:

The answer is found in the text.

The answer is easily found within a single statement or paragraph.

Wording:

The wording of the question is found in the text and may be repeated in the answer.

The answer may use the exact wording in the text.

Content:

The answer is usually a definition, a fact, or a detail from the text.

Format:

The question-answer format is usually multiple-choice.

Think and Search

Source:

The answer is found in the text.

The answer is found in more than one statement, paragraph, or section of the text.

Wording:

The wording of the question may or may not be found in the text.

The answer may or may not use the wording in the text.

Content:

The answer may require inferring or summarizing from information given in the text.

The answer may address the main idea of the text.

Format:

The question-answer format may be multiple-choice or short answer.

IN MY HEAD

Author and Me

Source:

The answer is based on my own knowledge and experience.

The answer combines an understanding of the text with my own knowledge or experience. It may connect to other texts I have read.

Wording:

The wording of the question is unlikely to be found in the text.

The answer may or may not use wording in the text. The answer may refer to or draw on points made in the text.

Content:

The answer is a narrative inferred from or based on information given in the text.

The answer addresses the main idea or theme of the text.

Format:

The question-answer format may be multiple-choice, short answer, or extended response (essay).

On My Own

Source:

The answer is based on my own knowledge and experience.

The answer is independent of the text. It is related to the general topic of the text but comes from my own experience, knowledge, and reading.

Wording:

The wording of the question is not found in the text.

The answer will not use wording in the text.

Content:

The answer is a personal narrative (explanation, opinion, description) related to the general topic or theme of the text.

Format:

The question-answer format is usually short answer or extended response (essay).

Directions: Reread the passage on page 3. Answer the questions and identify the QAR. On the next page, write the strategies you used to find the answers.

QUESTION / ANSWER / QAR

1. What did audiences of the antislavery speakers criticize?

   QAR: _____

2. What were some rights women lacked in the 1800s?

   QAR: _____

3. In this passage, the term *abolitionists* refers to what?

   QAR: _____

4. What is our society's attitude toward women's rights today?

   QAR: _____

Concept Lesson 1

STRATEGY

1.

2.

3.

4.

Concept Lesson 1

Directions: Write a short-answer question about the text on page 3 for each type of QAR. Then tell why the question represents that QAR.

Right There

Question	Answer	Why this is a Right There QAR

Think and Search

Question	Answer	Why this is a Think and Search QAR

Author and Me

Question	Answer	Why this is an Author and Me QAR

On My Own

Question	Answer	Why this is an On My Own QAR

Concept Lesson 1

Directions: Write four new questions about the text on page 3 in the spaces provided. (Do not fill in the answers.) When instructed to do so, exchange your *Student Activity Book* with a partner and answer each other's questions.

Partner's Name: _____

Directions: Answer each question, identify the QAR, and explain how you know what kind of QAR it is.

1.

   Answer:

   QAR:

   How do you know:

2.

   Answer:

   QAR:

   How do you know:

Concept Lesson 1

3.

   Answer:

   QAR:

   How do you know:

4.

   Answer:

   QAR:

   How do you know:

Directions: Read this passage from *Sue at the Field Museum*.

Sue the T-Rex

The first *T. rex* specimen was found in 1900. Since then, only seven skeletons that are more than half complete have been discovered. Of these, Sue is the largest, most complete, and best preserved *T. rex* ever found. Most of Sue's bones are in excellent condition and have a high degree of surface detail. Sixty-seven million years after her death, it is still possible to see fine details showing where muscles, tendons, and other soft tissues rested against or attached to the bone. Sue's completeness, combined with the exquisite preservation of the bones, makes her an invaluable scientific resource, permitting highly detailed study of *T. rex* anatomy.

In the summer of 1990, Sue Hendrickson was working as a fossil hunter with a commercial fossil-collecting team near Faith, South Dakota. On August 12 most of the team went into town to get a flat tire fixed and to take a short break from the heat. Sue stayed behind to look for fossils. She hiked over to some sandstone bluffs that had previously caught her attention. Within minutes she spotted some bone fragments on the ground. She scanned the cliffs above to find out where the fragments had fallen from and saw dinosaur bones—big ones. She climbed up the cliff for a better look at the bones, and saw they were huge. She thought she had found a *T. rex*, and when the team returned, they confirmed her find and promptly named it "Sue" in her honor.

Soon after Sue was discovered, her bones became the center of a dispute. Who owned the fossil?

To dig up dinosaurs, you always need the landowner's permission. But in Sue's case it was unclear whose land it was because . . . the bones were found on land that was part of a Sioux Indian reservation, BUT . . . the land belonged to a private rancher, BUT . . . the rancher was part Sioux, and his land was held in trust by the U.S. government. While people argued about who owned Sue, the bones were safely locked away in storerooms at the South Dakota School of Mines and Technology. In the end, a judge decided that Sue was held in trust by the U.S. government for the rancher on whose property the skeleton had been found. The rancher, in turn, decided to sell Sue at public auction.

Following the long custody battle, Sue was sold at Sotheby's auction house in New York on October 4, 1997. Just eight minutes after the bidding started, the Field Museum of Chicago purchased Sue for nearly $8.4 million—the most money ever paid for a fossil. On May 17, 2000, the Field Museum unveiled Sue, the largest, most complete, and best preserved *T. rex* fossil yet discovered.

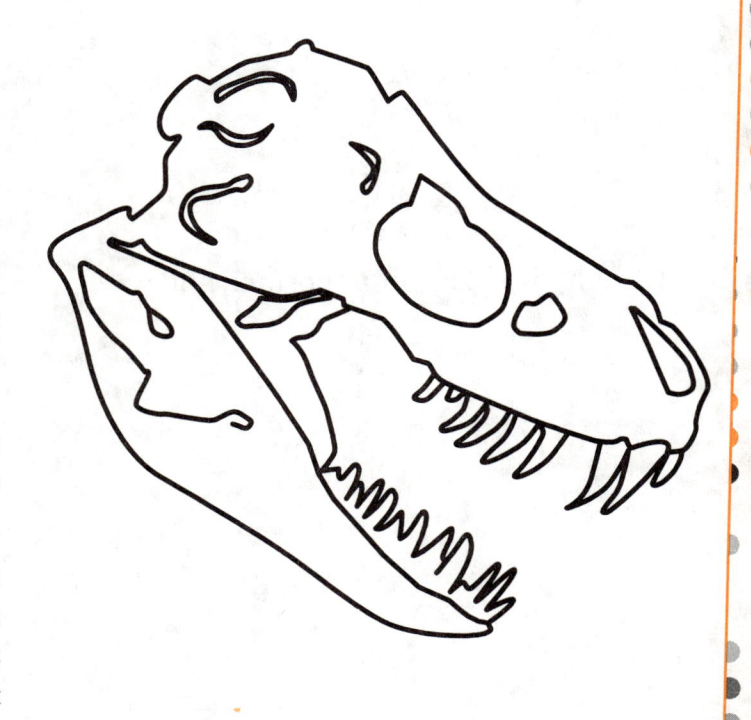

Directions: Answer the questions below about the text on page 11. Then, identify the text structure and the strategy you used to find the answer.

QUESTION / ANSWER

1. Who found Sue?

   A. A rancher
   B. A hike
   C. A professional fossil hunter
   D. None of the above

2. What happened after Sue was found?

   A. The ownership of the bones was contested.
   B. The bones were temporarily stored at a university.
   C. The bones were put on display at a museum.
   D. All of the above.

3. Why was the ownership of the bones unclear?

4. Why was Sue an important find?

TEXT STRUCTURE	STRATEGY
1.	1.
2.	2.
3.	3.
4.	4.

Concept Lesson 2

Directions: Write two short-answer Think and Search questions about the text on page 11. Then for each question, write the answer, identify the text structure, and tell why the QAR is Think and Search.

1.

   Answer:

   Text Structure:

   Why this is a Think and Search QAR:

2.

   Answer:

   Text Structure:

   Why this is a Think and Search QAR:

Directions: Write two new questions about the text on page 11 in the spaces provided. (Do not fill in the answers.) When instructed to do so, exchange your *Student Activity Book* with a partner and answer each other's questions.

Partner's Name: _____

Directions: Answer each question, identify the QAR, explain how you know what kind of QAR it is, and identify the strategies you used.

1.

Answer:

QAR:

How do you know:

Strategies for finding the answer:

2.

Answer:

QAR:

How do you know:

Strategies for finding the answer:

Concept Lesson 2

In My Head Sample Questions

1. **Author and Me: Text to Self**
   - How would you feel if you were the main character?
   - Compare your experience with that of someone in the story.
   - How does the situation today reflect the outcome of events described in the text?

   Notes:

2. **Author and Me: Text to Text**
   - Compare the main character with a character in another text you have read. How is he or she the same or different?

   Notes:

3. **Author and Me: Text to Themes**
   - What is the theme of the story?
   - What do you think was the author's primary message to the reader?

   Notes:

4. **On My Own**
   - Do you think women have full civil rights? Why or why not? Explain your conclusion.
   - Describe a time when you were scared. Why were you frightened? What happened?

   Notes:

Directions: Read this excerpt from *The Red Badge of Courage: An Episode of the American Civil War* by Stephen Crane. Then answer the questions on the next page.

The Red Badge of Courage

The cold passed reluctantly from the earth, and the retiring fogs revealed an army stretched out on the hills, resting. As the landscape changed from brown to green, the army awakened, and began to tremble with eagerness at the noise of rumors....

Once a certain tall soldier developed virtues and went resolutely to wash a shirt. He came flying back from a brook waving his garment bannerlike. He was swelled with a tale he had heard from a reliable friend, who had heard it from a truthful cavalryman, who had heard it from his trustworthy brother, one of the orderlies at division headquarters. He adopted the important air of a herald in red and gold. "We're goin' t' move t' morrah—sure," he said pompously to a group in the company street. "We're goin' 'way up the river, cut across, an' come around in behint 'em."

To his attentive audience he drew a loud and elaborate plan of a very brilliant campaign. When he had finished, the blue-clothed men scattered into small arguing groups between the rows of squat brown huts.... "It's a lie! that's all it is—a thunderin' lie!" said another private loudly. His smooth face was flushed, and his hands were thrust sulkily into his trousers' pockets. He took the matter as an affront to him. "I don't believe the derned old army's ever going to move. We're set. I've got ready to move eight times in the last two weeks, and we ain't moved yet."

The tall soldier felt called upon to defend the truth of a rumor he himself had introduced. He and the loud one came near to fighting over it....

Many of the men engaged in a spirited debate. One outlined in a peculiarly lucid manner all the plans of the commanding general. He was opposed by men who advocated that there were other plans of campaign. They clamored at each other, numbers making futile bids for the popular attention. Meanwhile, the soldier who had fetched the rumor bustled about with much importance....

There was a youthful private who listened with eager ears to the words of the tall soldier and to the varied comments of his comrades. After receiving a fill of discussions concerning marches and attacks, he went to his hut and crawled through an intricate hole that served it as a door. He wished to be alone with some new thoughts that had lately come to him....

The youth was in a little trance of astonishment. So they were at last going to fight. On the morrow, perhaps, there would be a battle, and he would be in it. For a time he was obliged to labor to make himself believe. He could not accept with assurance an omen that he was about to mingle in one of those great affairs of the earth.

He had, of course, dreamed of battles all his life—of vague and bloody conflicts that had thrilled him with their sweep and fire. In visions he had seen himself in many struggles. He had imagined peoples secure in the shadow of his eagle-eyed prowess. But awake he had regarded battles as crimson blotches on the pages of the past. He had put them as things of the bygone with his thought-images of heavy crowns and high castles. There was a portion of the world's history which he had regarded as the time of wars, but it, he thought, had been long gone over the horizon and had disappeared forever.

Directions: Answer the following questions about the text on page 17. Indicate the type of QAR, where you found the answer, and the strategies you used to find the answer.

QUESTION / ANSWER / QAR

1. Describe how the soldiers responded to the rumor of battle and how you react to rumors or gossip that you hear.

   QAR: _____

2. The "youth" in this passage "was about to mingle in one of those great affairs of the earth." Compare this "great affair" with an event in another story you have read.

   QAR: _____

3. In this passage, one of the author's themes is
   A. how the uncertainty of war affected the soldiers
   B. people will believe anything they hear
   C. the soldiers were not afraid to die
   D. the virtues of bravery

   QAR: _____

4. What would it be like to be a soldier facing battle? What would your thoughts and concerns be?

   QAR: _____

SOURCE	STRATEGY
1.	1.
2.	2.
3.	3.
4.	4.

Directions: Write two short-answer In My Head questions about the text on page 17. Then write the answers and why the QAR categories are In My Head.

Question	Answer	Why this is an In My Head QAR

Question	Answer	Why this is an In My Head QAR

Directions: Write two new questions about the text on page 17 in the spaces provided. (Do not fill in the answers.) When instructed to do so, exchange your *Student Activity Book* with a partner and answer each other's questions.

Partner's Name: _____

Directions: Answer each question, identify the QAR, and explain how you know what type of QAR it is.

1.

Answer:

QAR:

How do you know:

2.

Answer:

QAR:

How do you know:

Test-Taking Strategies

Before you read the text…
- Read the test questions first.
- Scan for key words in the text.
- Skim first and last sentences; read the text quickly to find the main idea.

As you read…
- Circle, underline, or highlight key words or phrases.
- Identify important information and make notes.
- Predict what will happen next.
- Connect to the text. Ask yourself: What do I already know about this topic? What else have I read about this topic? Have I experienced something similar?
- Identify the theme.

Before you answer the question…
- Reread the question.
- Identify the QAR.
- Reread or skim the text.
- Scan your notes and words or phrases that you highlighted in the text.
- Brainstorm an answer and briefly note your thoughts. For an essay question, make a short outline of your answer.

For your answer…
- Summarize, infer, draw conclusions, or make connections.
- Support your answer with details from the text.
- Write complete sentences. Use conventional grammar, punctuation, and spelling.
- Pace yourself. Don't spend too much time on any one answer.

Directions: Read the following excerpt from *Ellen Foster* by Kaye Gibbons.

Chapter 1, Part 1

When I was little I would think of ways to kill my daddy…

He drank his own self to death the year after the County moved me out… And I can say for a fact that I am better off now than when he was alive.

I live in a clean brick house and mostly I am left to myself. When I start to carry an odor I take a bath and folks tell me how sweet I look.

There is a plenty to eat here and if we run out of something we just go to the store and get some more. I had me a egg sandwich for breakfast, mayonnaise on both sides. And I may fix me another one for lunch.

Two years ago I did not have much of anything. Not that I live in the lap of luxury now but I am proud for the schoolbus to pick me up here every morning. My stylish well-groomed self standing in the front yard with the grass green and the hedge bushes square.

I figure I made out pretty good considering the rest of my family is either dead or crazy…

Oh but I do remember when I was scared. Everything was so wrong like somebody had knocked something loose and my family was shaking itself to death. Some wild ride broke and the one in charge strolled off and let us spin and shake and fly off the rail. And they both died tired of the wild crazy spinning and wore out and sick…

Even my mama's skin looked tired of holding in her weak self. She would prop herself up by the refrigerator and watch my daddy go round the table swearing at all who did him wrong. She looked all sad in her face like it was all her fault.

She comes home from the hospital sometimes. If I was her I would stay there. All laid up in the air conditioning with folks patting your head and bringing you fruit baskets.

Oh no. She comes in and he lets into her right away. Carrying on. Set up in his E-Z lounger like he is King for a Day. You bring me this or that he might say.

She comes in the door and he asks about supper right off. What does she have planned? he wants to know. Wouldn't he like to know what I myself have planned?… More like a big mean baby than a grown man…

Big wind-up toy of a man. He is just too sorry to talk back to even if he is my daddy. And she is too limp and too sore to get up the breath to push the words out to stop it all. She just stands there and lets him work out his evil on her.

Get in the kitchen and fix me something to eat. I had to cook the whole time you was gone, he tells her.

And that was some lie he made up. Cook for his own self. Ha. If I did not feed us both we had to go into town and get take-out chicken. I myself was looking forward to something fit to eat but I was not about to say anything.

Directions: Complete this chart as you work together with your peers and teacher.

QUESTION / ANSWER / QAR

1. The relationship Ellen had with her dad was that
    A. he took care of her
    B. she took care of him
    C. she lived away from him
    D. she admired him

    QAR: _____

2. What has happened to Ellen in the past two years?

    QAR: _____

3. Compare Ellen's old life with her new life.

    QAR: _____

4. What does Ellen value most in life?

    QAR: _____

STRATEGY

1.

2.

3.

4.

Directions: Read more from *Ellen Foster*. Then answer the questions on pages 27 through 29.

Chapter 1, Part 2

Nobody yells after anybody to do this or that here.

My new mama lays out the food and we all take a turn to dish it out. Then we eat and have a good time. Toast or biscuits with anything you please. Eggs any style. Corn cut off the cob the same day we eat it. I keep my elbows off the table and wipe my mouth like a lady. …When everybody is done eating my new mama puts the dishes in a thing, shuts the door, cuts on it, and Wa-La they are clean

My mama does not say a word about being tired or sore. She did ask who kept everything so clean and he took the credit. I do not know who he thinks he fooled. I knew he lied and my mama did too. She just asked to be saying something.

Mama puts the food out on the table and he wants to know what I am staring at. At you humped over your plate like one of us is about to snatch it from you. You old hog. But I do not say it.

Why don't you eat? he wants to know.

I don't have an appetite, I say back.

Well, you better eat. Your mama looks like this might be her last supper.

He is so sure he's funny that he laughs at his own self…

Now at my new mama's I lay up late in the day and watch the rain fall outside. Not one thing is pressing on me to get done here.

I have a bag of candy to eat on. One piece at a time. Make it last. All I got left to do is eat supper and wash myself.

Look around my room. It is so nice.

When I accumulate enough money I plan to get some colored glass things that you dangle from the window glass. I lay here and feature how that would look. I already got pink checkerboard curtains with dingleballs around the edges. My new mama sewed them for me. She also sewed matching sacks that I cram my pillows into every morning.

Everything matches. It is all so neat and clean…

The yelling makes my mama jump and if she was asleep she is awake now. Grits her teeth every time he calls out damn this or that. The more he drinks the less sense he makes.

By the time the dog races come on he's stretched out on the bathroom floor and can't get up. I know I need to go in there and poke him. Same thing every Saturday…

I get up and go in there and tell him to get up that folks got to come in here and do their business.

He can go lay in the truck.

He just grunts and grabs at my ankle and misses.

Get on up I say again to him. You got to be firm when he is like this. He'd lay there and rot if I let him so I nudge him with my foot. I will not touch my hands to him. Makes me want to heave my own self seeing him pull himself up on the sink. He zig-zags out through the living room and

Chapter 1, Part 2 (continued)

I guess he makes it out the door. I don't hear him fall down the steps.

And where did she come from? Standing in the door looking at it all.

Get back in bed, I say to mama.

Mama's easy to tend to. She goes back in the bedroom. Not a bit of trouble. Just stiff and hard to move around. I get her back in the bed and tell her he's outside for the night. She starts to whimper and I say it is no reason to cry. But she will wear herself out crying.

I ought to lock him out.

A grown man that should be bringing her food to nibble on and books to look at. No but he is taking care of his own self tonight. Just like she is not sick or kin to him.

A storm is coming up. And I will lay here with my mama until I see her chest rise up and sink down regular. Deep and regular and far away from the man in the truck.

Directions: Answer the questions below and on the next two pages. Identify the QAR categories and the test-taking strategies you used.

1. Ellen is most upset that her father
   - A. doesn't work
   - B. abuses her mother
   - C. does not take care of her mother
   - D. does not take care of her

   QAR: _____

   Test-Taking Strategy:

2. Describe Ellen's feelings toward her father during the scene when her mother has returned home.

   QAR: _____
   Test-Taking Strategy:

3. What role has Ellen taken on in her birth family and why?

   QAR: _____
   Test-Taking Strategy:

4. Ellen's feelings toward her father could best be described as
   A. anger
   B. pity
   C. disgust
   D. A and B
   E. A and C

   QAR: _____
   Test-Taking Strategy:

5. Describe the stability and simple pleasures of Ellen's new life.

   QAR: _____
   Test-Taking Strategy:

6. If Ellen went to your school, what would you think of her? Give specific examples and reasons.

   QAR: _____
   Test-Taking Strategy:

Concept Lesson 4

7. Ellen's new life is like her old one because
   A. no one yells
   B. her mother takes care of her
   C. she has plenty to eat
   D. she lives in a messy place
   E. none of the above

   QAR: _____

   Test-Taking Strategy:

8. How does Ellen's birth mother react to her husband?

   QAR: _____

   Test-Taking Strategy:

9. Compare and contrast Ellen's new life with her old life. Use details from the story to support your answer.

   QAR: _____

   Test-Taking Strategy:

10. Ellen had to struggle to survive in her birth family. Describe a personal experience in which you struggled for success, happiness, stability, approval, or some other goal.

    QAR: _____

    Test-Taking Strategy:

Directions: Read the following article by Marcella J. Kehus.

The Complexities of Cloning

Before 1996, few people had actually considered cloning a real possibility beyond something you might read about or see in a science fiction movie. But in July of that year, when Dolly the ewe (baby sheep) was born as a clone of her mother, some great debates began that are still raging in many areas. Cloning, or the creating of a living replica from DNA from a body cell, took quite a long time to develop before it actually worked with Dolly as its first success. Now people from politicians to religious leaders to scientists and the general public continue to argue over whether this technology should be applied to humans. The basic debate comes down to: Should we or should we not allow the cloning of human beings? And, if we do so, what are the possible results?

Now that the procedure for cloning has been discovered, it seems only a matter of time before it is applied to humans. This is where a number of people, specialists and general citizens alike, have serious concerns. One of their primary concerns, which often comes up with every new technology, are the number of ways that such a technology might be abused. For example, what if a certain group wanted to use cloning to create an army of exact duplicate soldiers or creatures to carry out their evil deeds? And, because cloning can include genetic engineering, or selecting just the right genes to create a certain kind of being (strong, green eyes, etc.), the idea of creating a look-alike super-human race reminds people quickly of the terrible possibilities of Hitler-like beliefs if given the power of cloning.

There are lesser kinds of abuses that the power of human cloning could inspire. Perhaps a former football player got his career cut short due to an injury; what would keep him from creating a clone of himself to play and become the star he always wanted to be? Cloning could become a fashionable way for other conceited people to just re-create themselves and the result may be a child who is never given a chance to become an individual.

On the other hand, there are impressive possibilities when it comes to human cloning. First, cloning is another possible solution for couples who are otherwise unable to have children of their own. In fact, the medical solutions made possible by clones are numerous including the supplying of life-saving transplant organs or bone marrow by cloned family members that would automatically match. And, when coupled with genetic engineering, cloning may allow us to create better humans as we discover more and more about disease and aging and produce clones who are better-equipped to survive.

Certainly, the possibilities of human cloning are scientifically possible. Yet, as with other new developments, one must carefully consider the possible outcomes—both good and bad. Ultimately, we as a society will make the decision as to whether human cloning's benefits outweigh its possible abuses and where we go from here.

Directions: Answer the following questions about the article on page 30 and identify each QAR.

1. According to the article, what "great debate" started in 1996?

   QAR: _____

2. What are other arguments against cloning that are not mentioned in the article?

   QAR: _____

3. Who is involved in the debate about human cloning?

   QAR: _____

4. What do you think is the strongest reason given for human cloning? Why?

   QAR: _____

5. What do you think is the strongest reason against human cloning? Why?

   QAR: _____

6. What are three different ways that individuals might benefit from human cloning?

   QAR: _____

7. Who do you think will make the final decision about whether or not human cloning is allowed?

   QAR: _____

Essay-Writing Tips, Part 1

- Before you start writing, identify the QAR.

- Create a short outline of your main thesis or idea and two or three main points that support your thesis. If you're stuck, do some brainstorming.

- Restate the question as a thesis or opening line(s).

- Answer all parts of the question. Check off each part as you go.

- For each part of the answer, note the specific part in the text that supports it.

- Include an introduction, at least two body paragraphs, and a conclusion.

- Present your ideas in a logical way. What comes first, second, third? What is your conclusion?

- If you have time, reread your essay to correct spelling, punctuation, or grammatical errors.

Directions: Reread the passage on page 30. Then choose a side for or against human cloning and write an essay to convince your audience to believe as you do.

Directions: Read "The Bungee Lunge" on pages 36 and 37. As you read, write five during reading questions in the spaces below. Identify the QAR that each question represents.

1.

   QAR: _____

2.

   QAR: _____

3.

   QAR: _____

4.

   QAR: _____

5.

   QAR: _____

Booster Lesson 1

Directions: Read this article by Karen McNulty.

The Bungee Lunge

Here's your giant rubber band. Now jump! It's only a 10-story plunge—and science will spring you back.

The Science Behind the Bounce

Ready?

When standing high on a jump platform, you have lots of potential (stored) energy.

Jump!

Leap off and your potential energy is converted to kinetic energy, the energy of motion. For a few seconds, you experience free fall, until there's no more slack in the cord.

Stret – t – ch

Then the cord starts to stretch. This stores the energy of your fall in the cord.

Bounce

This stored energy springs you back up. You fall and bounce again… and again…

Phew!

Each bounce disperses some of your energy, so eventually you stop. You'll have to hang around until someone lowers you to a raft or the ground.

You're hanging onto the railing of a bridge, 46 m above the river. Your friends on the bank below seem awfully small; looking at them makes you dizzy. Someone standing behind you is counting down "Three…two…one!" Defying every sane notion in your brain, you leap—headfirst.

The 100 km/h fall toward the water terrifies you. But just as you close your eyes for the icy plunge, something happens: You bounce back!

Better thank your lucky *bungee cord*—that wrist-thick band of latex rubber strapped to your ankles and anchored to the bridge. Because it was the right length, it kept you high and dry. And because it stret-t-t-ched and recoiled—giving you a few good bounces—it used up the energy of your fall so you didn't get torn limb from limb. Phew!

Those who have done it say it's the thrill of a lifetime—"a natural high." Others call it crazy. But everyone knows it as "bungee jumping," the sport springing up (and down) across the nation.

At least one group of people has been "bungee jumping" for ages: the men of Pentecost Island in the South Pacific. They make cords from elastic vines, lash them to their ankles, and plunge off wooden towers into pits of softened earth. For these islanders, jumping is a springtime ritual, meant to demonstrate courage and supposedly ensure a plentiful yam harvest.

In North America, jumpers take the bungee plunge just for the excitement of it. Scott Bergman, who runs a bungee-jumping company in California, explains the appeal. "It's a feeling of having absolutely no control—and loving it."

And it doesn't take any skill. Just $75 to $100 and *faith*—in physics. It's a simple physics equation, after all, that let's "jump masters" like Bergman determine how far the cord will stretch when you take the plunge—whether it will stretch too far.

Booster Lesson 1

The Bungee Lunge (continued)

Weighing the Odds

The major variables are the stretchiness, or *elasticity*, of the cord—predetermined by the manufacturer—and the jumper's weight. As you might guess, "the heavier you are, the more the cord is going to stretch," says physicist Peter Brancazio.

By weighing customers (they don't just ask), using the equation, and adjusting cords, jump masters have bounced thousands to safety. (There have been some deaths—usually caused by frayed cords or other faulty equipment.)

Jump experts can even adjust the cords to give their clients custom-made thrills. "When we jump off bridges in California," says Bergman, "we ask the people if they want to just touch the water, dunk their heads in, or go all the way. We can really get it that exact."

Really? "I wouldn't trust them," says Brancazio, "but I guess they can."

If, for example, Bergman calculates that you'll crack your skull on a rock in the river, he can shorten your cord. "That starts the stretch at a higher point off the ground," says Brancazio.

Or you can jump with two cords. "In that case," says Brancazio, your weight is "equally divided between the cords so each stretches half as far."

Chances are, you'll scream just as hard with fear and delight.

Directions: Write a short answer to the following questions based on the article on pages 36 and 37 and identify the QAR for each.

1. Explain how energy is stored and released in a bungee cord.

   QAR: _____

2. Summarize the points of view of the two experts (Scott Bergman and Peter Brancazio) quoted in the article. Why might they have different perspectives on bungee jumping?

   QAR: _____

3. Would you ever consider bungee jumping? What would be your major considerations in making a decision?

   QAR: _____

4. Compare bungee jumping in the South Pacific to California.

   QAR: _____

5. Compare the during reading questions you wrote on page 35 with the questions above. What types of QAR categories are there? Which of your questions prepared you for the questions asked above, if any?

   QAR: _____

Tips for Using Textbooks

Look at text features:
- Headings and subheadings
- Summaries (main idea, key points)
- Terms and their definitions
- Words bolded or highlighted in the text
- Captions for illustrations

Use previewing techniques:
- Preview comprehension questions or exercises at the end.
- Skim the first and last sentences of each paragraph.

Take notes and ask questions:
- Restate definitions and explanations in your own words.
- Connect to the text: What do I already know? What do I want to learn?
- Restate or paraphrase questions in your own words.

Directions: Read this passage from *American History: The Early Years to 1877.*

The Women's Rights Movement

Guide to Reading

Main Idea

Emboldened by their work in the antislavery movement, many women fought to improve their own status in society.

Read to Learn...

* why women became unhappy with their positions in the mid-1800s
* how working in the antislavery movement prepared women to fight for their own rights
* what arguments opponents used against the women's rights movement

Terms to Know

* abolitionist
* suffrage

Women took a special interest in the antislavery movement. As they fought for social reform for African Americans, they realized that they also lacked full social and political rights. When women such as Angelina and Sarah Grimké tried to participate actively in the antislavery movement, they often met resistance. As a result, many abolitionists became crusaders for women's rights.

Equal rights for women would require major reform. In the 1800s women actually had fewer rights than in colonial times. They had few political or legal rights. Women could not vote. They could not hold public office. A woman's husband owned all her property.

Antislavery Movement Gives Women a Boost

Women from New England to Ohio joined the antislavery societies. They worked hard, gathering signatures on thousands of petitions to send to Congress. They also read about and discussed the abuses of slavery. Many saw similarities between the treatment of enslaved persons and women.

In her book *Woman in the Nineteenth Century,* journalist **Margaret Fuller** observed that "there exists in the minds of men a tone of feeling toward women as towards slaves." Abolitionists Angelina and Sarah Grimké confronted this feeling when they spoke to antislavery groups. Audiences did not criticize their stand on slavery. They did, though, question their right to speak in public.

As a result, the Grimkés soon found themselves in the midst of "an entirely new contest—a contest for the rights of woman." Sarah wrote that "all I ask... is that [men] will take their feet from off our necks and permit us to stand upright."

The Women's Rights Movement

Their involvement in the antislavery movement and other reform movements gave women roles outside their homes and families. They learned valuable skills, such as organizing, working

The Women's Rights Movement (continued)

together, and speaking in public. Eventually they used these skills to further their own cause—the women's rights movement.

In 1840 nine women from the United States attended the World Anti-Slavery Convention in **London.** When the women arrived at the convention, however, the male delegates barred them from participating. The women and some male allies protested. On the first day of the convention, delegates debated the situation.

Clergy at the convention considered it improper for women to participate. Other male delegates declared women "unfit for public or business meetings." In the end, the majority of delegates decided that women could not take part in discussions. Instead, the women delegates would have to sit in the gallery behind a curtain.

Humiliated and angry, two of the women, Lucretia Coffin Mott and Elizabeth Cady Stanton, spent hours after the meetings talking about women's position in society. They realized that they could not bring about social change if they themselves lacked social and political rights. Stanton and Mott "resolved to hold a convention as soon as we returned home, and form a society to advocate the rights of women."

The Seneca Falls Convention

Eight years passed before the two friends organized their convention. On July 19, 1848, the first women's rights convention opened in Seneca Falls, New York. Both male and female delegates attended the convention. The delegates issued the Seneca Falls Declaration, which proclaimed that "all men and women are created equal."

Then the declaration listed several resolutions. One of them demanded suffrage, or the right to vote, for women. Even supporters of women's rights hesitated to pass this bold demand. Mott exclaimed, "Oh, Lizzie, thou will make us ridiculous! We must go slowly." But Stanton refused to withdraw the resolution. After much heated debate, it passed by a narrow margin.

The Seneca Falls Convention marked the beginning of an organized women's rights movement. Following the convention, women did not achieve all of their demands. They did, however, overcome some obstacles. Many states passed laws permitting women to own their own property and keep their earnings. Many men and women, though, continued to oppose the movement. Most politicians ignored or acted hostile to the issue of women's rights.

The Women's Rights Movement (continued)

Assessment

Check for Understanding
1. Define suffrage.
2. Why did women become unhappy with their position in the mid-1800s? About what areas of their daily lives were they most concerned?

Critical Thinking
3. **Comparing and Contrasting.** Contrast the views of the men and women who opposed the women's rights movement with those who supported it.

4. **Identifying Relationships.** Re-create the diagram shown here, and list how women's work in the antislavery movement prepared them to fight for their own rights.

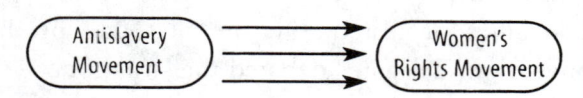

Antislavery Movement → Women's Rights Movement

Interdisciplinary Activity

5. **Citizenship.** Are women today denied any rights that men have? Draw up an agenda for a new Seneca Falls Convention listing topics for discussion.

Directions: Read "The Women's Rights Movement" on pages 40 and 41 and answer the questions from the Assessment section on page 42. Identify the type of QAR each question represents.

1.

   QAR: _____

2.

   QAR: _____

3.

   QAR: _____

4.

   QAR: _____

5.

   Write your agenda on a separate sheet or in your "QAR Reflections Journal."

   QAR: _____

Booster Lesson 2

Directions: Read this letter to President Franklin D. Roosevelt.

Dear Mr. President

Phila., Pa.
November 26, 1934

Honorable Franklin D. Roosevelt
Washington, D.C.

Dear Mr. President:

I am forced to write to you because we find ourselves in a very serious condition. For the last three or four years we have had depression and suffered with my family and little children severely. Now Since the Home Owners Loan Corporation opened up, I have been going up there in order to save my home, because there has been unemployment in my house for more than three years. You can imagine that I and my family have suffered from lack of water supply in my house for more than two years. Last winter I did not have coal and the pipes burst in my house and therefore could not make heat in the house. Now winter is here again and we are suffering of cold, no water in the house, and we are facing to be forced out of the house, because I have no money to move or pay so much money as they want when after making settlement. I am mother of little children, am sick and losing my health, and we are eight people in the family, and where can I go when I don't have money because no one is working in my house. The Home Loan Corporation wants $42. a month rent or else we will have to be on the street. I am living in this house for about ten years and when times were good we would put our last cent in the house and now I have no money, no home and no wheres to go. I beg of you to please help me and my family and little children for the sake of a sick mother and a suffering family to give this your immediate attention so we will not be forced to move or put out in the street.

Waiting and Hoping that you will act quickly.
Thanking you very much I remain

Mrs. E. L.

Booster Lesson 3

Directions: Read this excerpt from a speech by Robert Kennedy.

On the Death of Dr. Martin Luther King

This speech was given by Robert F. Kennedy on April 4, 1968, shortly after Dr. Martin Luther King, Jr. had been assassinated. At the time, Robert Kennedy was a U.S. Senator leading a race for the presidency, but he was assassinated a few months later.

Martin Luther King dedicated his life to love and to justice between fellow human beings. He died in the cause of that effort. In this difficult day, in this difficult time for the United States, it's perhaps well to ask what kind of a nation we are and what direction we want to move in.

For those of you who are black—considering the evidence evidently is that there were white people who were responsible—you can be filled with bitterness, and with hatred, and a desire for revenge.

We can move in that direction as a country, in greater polarization—black people amongst blacks, and white amongst whites, filled with hatred toward one another. Or we can make an effort, as Martin Luther King did, to understand and to comprehend, and replace that violence, that stain of bloodshed that has spread across our land, with an effort to understand, compassion and love.

For those of you who are black and are tempted to be filled with hatred and mistrust of the injustice of such an act, against all white people, I would only say that I can also feel in my own heart the same kind of feeling. I had a member of my family killed, but he was killed by a white man.

But we have to make an effort in the United States, we have to make an effort to understand, to get beyond these rather difficult times.

My favorite poet was Aeschylus. He once wrote: "Even in our sleep, pain which cannot forget falls drop by drop upon the heart, until, in our own despair, against our will, comes wisdom through the awful grace of God."

What we need in the United States is not division; what we need in the United States is not hatred; what we need in the United States is not violence and lawlessness, but is love and wisdom, and compassion toward one another, and a feeling of justice toward those who still suffer within our country, whether they be white or whether they be black.

So I ask you tonight to return home, to say a prayer for the family of Martin Luther King, yeah that's true, but more importantly to say a prayer for our own country, which all of us love—a prayer for understanding and that compassion of which I spoke. We can do well in this country. We will have difficult times. We've had difficult times in the past. And we will have difficult times in the future. It is not the end of violence; it is not the end of lawlessness; and it's not the end of disorder.

But the vast majority of white people and the vast majority of black people in this country want to live together, want to improve the quality of our life, and want justice for all human beings that abide in our land.

Let us dedicate ourselves to what the Greeks wrote so many years ago: to tame the savageness of man and make gentle the life of this world.

Let us dedicate ourselves to that, and say a prayer for our country and for our people.

Directions: Read pages 44 and 45 and then answer the following questions. Identify the QAR after your answer.

1. Compare and contrast the audience, purpose, and writing style of the two passages.

   QAR: _____

2. If you were President Roosevelt, how would you have responded to Mrs. E. L.'s letter? Why?

   QAR: _____

3. What would have been your reaction to Robert F. Kennedy's speech at the time. Why?

   QAR: _____

Best-Answer Strategies

IN THE BOOK

Right There
- Reread.
- Scan for key words.
- Recall key facts or figures.

Think and Search
- Reread.
- Scan for key words.
- Skim first and last sentences.
- Identify important information.
- Look for specific examples.
- Identify characters or people, events, plot, problem and solutions, etc.
- Identify the main idea or theme.
- Predict what will happen next.

IN MY HEAD

Author and Me
- Reread.
- Skim first and last sentences.
- Connect to important information What do I already know about this subject?
- Connect to the characters or people and events in the text.
- Connect to the main idea or theme.
- Predict what will happen next.
- Connect to other texts. What have I read before on this same subject or with this same theme?

On My Own
- Reread.
- Connect to the general theme or topic.
- Connect to other texts. What have I read before on this same subject or with this same theme?

Directions: Read this passage from *Lasers* by Lynne Kelly and answer the questions on page 49.

How a Laser Beam Is Made

The first pulse laser was made by Theodore H. Maiman of the United States in 1960. He used a ruby rod to make a short flash of laser light. The method has been improved since then, but the idea is the same.

1. A rod of ruby, about the size of a finger is used. Real ruby is very expensive, but synthetic ruby can be used.
2. The ends of the ruby rod are ground so they are perfectly smooth and parallel to each other. Each end is painted silver to make mirrors, but one end receives a thinner layer of paint than the other. This means that this end is only partially reflective.
3. A flash tube is wrapped around the ruby rob and connected to a battery. The flash tube and battery act as the power source.
4. When the flash tube is switched on, it produces bright, white light. This excites, or increases, the energy level of chromium atoms in the ruby. Light is reflected back and forth along the rod.
5. After a fraction of a second, a bright flash of red laser light will come out of the end of the ruby rod.

When the flash tube is switched on, chromium atoms in the ruby rod absorb some of the light energy. These atoms then give out energy again in the form of colored light. Light beams given out from one sort of atom that has been excited in this way will all be identical.

These identical light beams reflect back and forth along the ruby rod from one mirror to the other. As they do so, they excite more atoms, which give off more light. This goes on until the light beam has grown strong enough to break through the thinner mirror. All the light beams emitted from the thinner mirror will be identical and coherent and will travel in a straight line. They will be a laser beam.

The name *laser* comes from the way in which a laser beam is made. It is a form of light that is the result of many reflections between the mirrors on the ends of the ruby rod. This causes the energy to increase, or amplify. The chromium atoms that give off the pure light beam have been excited, or stimulated, by the flash of light. The atoms give out, or emit, pure monochromatic light, which is a form of electromagnetic radiation.

So a laser beam is the result of Light Amplification by Stimulated Emission of Radiation.

Directions: Answer the following questions about the text on page 48.

1. Which list includes the items used in generating laser light?
    A. ruby rod, flash tube, light switch
    B. synthetic ruby, mirrors, chromium atoms
    C. ruby rod, flash tube, battery
    D. ruby rod, reflective coating, flash tube, battery

2. What is the purpose of the mirrors at each end of the rod?
    A. They intensify the energy of the light beams as the light beams reflect back and forth between the mirrors.
    B. The protect the ends of the ruby rod as the high energy light beams travel back and forth.
    C. They decrease the level of energy of the chromium atoms in the ruby.
    D. None of the above.

3. What is the purpose of the flash tube and battery?
    A. They hold the ruby rod in place.
    B. They excite the chromium atoms.
    C. They make the light beams coherent.
    D. They generate the power needed to produce the energy for the laser beam.

4. How is a laser beam made?

5. Choose question 1, 2, or 3 above and analyze each response (A, B, C, D). Is it correct, partially correct, or incorrect? Why? Identify a statement or section of the passage that supports your answer.

Booster Lesson 4

The Road Not Taken

Two roads diverged in a yellow wood,
And sorry I could not travel both
And be one traveler, long I stood
And looked down one as far as I could
To where it bent in the undergrowth;

Then took the other, as just as fair,
And having perhaps the better claim,
Because it was grassy and wanted wear;
Though as for that the passing there
Had worn them really about the same,

And both that morning equally lay
In leaves no step had trodden black.
Oh, I kept the first for another day!
Yet knowing how way leads on to way,
I doubted if I should ever come back.

I shall be telling this with a sigh
Somewhere ages and ages hence:
Two roads diverged in a wood, and I—
I took the one less traveled by,
And that has made all the difference.

by Robert Frost

Life

They told me that Life could be just what I made it—
    Life could be fashioned and worn like a gown;
I, the designer; mine the decision
    Whether to wear it with bonnet or crown.

And so I selected the prettiest pattern—
    Life should be made of the rosiest hue—
Something unique, and a bit out of fashion,
    One that perhaps would be chosen by few.

But other folks came and they leaned o'er my shoulder;
    Somebody questioned the ultimate cost;
Somebody tangled the thread I was using;
    One day I found that my scissors were lost.

And somebody claimed the material faded;
    Somebody said I'd be tired ere 'twas worn;
Somebody's fingers, too pointed and spiteful,
    Snatched at the cloth, and I saw it was torn.

Oh! somebody tried to do all the sewing,
    Wanting always to advise or condone.
Here is my life, the product of many;
    Where is that gown I could fashion—alone?

by Nan Terrell Reed

Directions: This test has two parts. When you're finished with Part 1, go on to Part 2.

Part 1

Directions: Read the poems on page 50 and 51. Then write five Author and Me questions (connecting self to text, text to text, and text to theme) about the poems.

Author and Me Questions
for "The Road Not Taken"

1.

2.

3.

4.

5.

Author and Me Questions
for "Life"

1.

2.

3.

4.

5.

Part 2

Directions: Answer the following questions about the two poems. Support your answers with details from the text. Identify the QAR after each answer.

1. In "The Road Not Taken," how did the narrator know that one of the roads was "less traveled by"?

    QAR: _____

2. Why did the narrator choose "the road less traveled by"?

    QAR: _____

3. How does the narrator feel about his decision?

    QAR: _____

Booster Lesson 5

Part 2, continued

4. What is the main idea or theme of "The Road Not Taken"?

   QAR: _____

5. In the poem "Life," what does the author compare life to? What did she want her life to be like?

   QAR: _____

6. Who is the "Somebody" referred to in the poem? What does this somebody do?

   QAR: _____

7. At the end of "Life," how does the narrator feel about her life?

   QAR: _____

Part 2, continued

8. What is the main idea or theme of "Life"?

   QAR: _____

9. Compare and contrast the narrators of the poems "The Road Not Taken" and "Life." What were they seeking? How did they feel about their "road taken" and "gown" at the end?

   QAR: _____

10. Compare and contrast the main ideas or themes in each poem. How are they different? How are they similar?

    QAR: _____

Solving Math Story Problems

Ask yourself...

1. **What is given?**

    Identify the information already stated or given in the problem.

2. **What am I supposed to figure out?**

    Restate the problem in terms of the unknown quantity.

3. **What is the math concept?**

    Identify the math concept or concepts you have to know. What have you already learned about this concept?

Do the work...

4. **Set up the problem.**

    > Always show your work. If you get an incorrect answer because of a computation error, you may get partial credit for setting up the problem correctly and showing how you got the answer.

5. **Do the calculation.**

6. **Select or write your answer.**

Booster Lesson 6

Directions: Answer the following question. Refer to the steps on page 56 if necessary.

In Malia's eighth-grade class, 3 out of 5 students are girls. In a class of 30 students, how many are girls?

A. 12

B. 18

C. 20

D. 22

1. What is given?

2. What am I supposed to figure out?

3. What is the math concept?

4. Set up the problem.

5. Do the calculation.

6. Select or write your answer.

Booster Lesson 6

Essay-Writing Tips, Part 2

Purpose

Identify the purpose of the essay:
- Narration
- Information
- Persuasion

Audience

Identify who you are writing for.

Text Type

Identify the text type:
- Formal essay
- Letter
- Editorial
- Newspaper or journal article
- Procedure
- Others

Evaluation

- **Development:** Are the ideas well developed? Does the essay have good supporting or descriptive details?
- **Organization:** Is the essay well organized? Does it have good transitions between ideas and paragraphs?
- **Use of language:** Is the sentence structure varied? Is descriptive or figurative language used effectively?
- **Mechanics:** Do grammatical, spelling, and punctuation errors interfere with understanding the content?

Directions: Complete this worksheet as you work together with your peers and teacher.

ESSAY-WRITING WORKSHEET

Write an article for the school newspaper explaining the benefits of playing computer games.

QAR:

Purpose:

Audience:

Text Type:

Brainstorm Ideas:

Outline:

Directions: With a partner, complete the worksheet. Then write your letter on the next page.

ESSAY-WRITING WORKSHEET

Think of a social issue affecting your school, neighborhood, or community (for example, pollution, noise, litter, homelessness, traffic, etc.). Write a letter to a public official describing the problem and asking for help. Explain what you think should be done to solve it and why.

QAR:

Purpose:

Audience:

Text Type:

Brainstorm Ideas:

Outline:

Directions: Use this page to write your letter.

Booster Lesson 7

Directions: Complete this worksheet and write your essay on the next page.

ESSAY-WRITING WORKSHEET

Imagine that you just saw on the news that computer scientists have perfected the technologies behind artificial intelligence and expect manufacturers to begin making robots soon with many—but not all—human capabilities.

Explain what you and your family members would like robots to do if you could buy them. What kinds of things do you think the robots should or should not do?

QAR:

Purpose:

Audience:

Text Type:

Brainstorm Ideas:

Outline:

Directions: Use this page to write your essay.

Directions: Read the following article from *Teen Vogue*, as told to Sarah Brown by Bess Judson. Then answer the questions on pages 66 through 69.

Survivor

I noticed the bump during the summer. I thought it was cool the way it moved when I swallowed, like a seed sliding under the skin of an orange slice. I made my mom touch it. "Maybe it's a tumor!" I said, laughing. "It's probably just a swollen gland or something. We'll get it checked out if it doesn't go away soon," she said, and sent me off to school.

I was psyched to go to college... My first semester at Hamilton, in upstate New York, was so much fun. I joined the rugby team and started feeling really good about myself again.

I didn't even think about my bump until Christmas break, when I switched from a pediatrician to a general practitioner, who gave me a complete physical. As soon as she felt the lump on my thyroid she sent me for a needle biopsy. I thought it was routine, although I was surprised I went for tests right away, instead of having to schedule an appointment.

And then I went back to school. The first night I was back, my doctor called. The tumor was malignant. I had cancer, and in one week, I was scheduled to have an operation to remove my thyroid. I hung up the phone thinking back to the pink fluid the doctor had removed from my bump during the biopsy. The liquid had looked so harmless inside the syringe, like water used to clean a red paintbrush.

I was totally petrified. As soon as you hear that word—*cancer*—no one knows what to say. Doctors don't really even know that much about it. All they can do is try to cut it out.

My surgeon told me I'd need to take two weeks off from school, which is what I'd planned to do. I spent two nights in the hospital, in and out of sleep. Every few hours a man who called himself the Vampire would wake me up to draw my blood. When I finally stood up to walk, I had to hold my mother's arm to stay on my feet. I inched through the halls, rolling my IV beside me like a fish dragging the rod that hooked it....

Your thyroid is a gland in your neck—the part of your body that regulates metabolism (the physical and chemical processes that essentially maintain life). It also controls a lot of your hormones, and for about a month, I was just miserable. After surgery, I had to wait awhile before I could start taking thyroid-replacement hormones (which simulate the way an actual thyroid works), so my entire hormonal makeup was out of whack. I was tired and I was sad and I would cry all the time about nothing. I was what they call hypothyroid—I felt sluggish and just really crummy.

When I was finally allowed to start taking Synthroid (synthetic thyroid hormones), I was expecting to feel normal right away—to go back to classes and to play rugby in the spring. They have to raise the hormones to the right levels incrementally, so in the beginning, I was taking only about half the level I am now. I went back to school, and I did play rugby, but let's just say I wasn't a huge success. I was so much slower than I'd been before. My friends were totally supportive—they couldn't believe I was playing at all. I signed up for a full course load, but I ended up having to drop a class. In the fall semester, I'd gotten some C's and a D... but this time, somehow, I got straight A's. I think I was just happy to be back, happy I was able to pull through and rebound...

Survivor (continued)

I spent the spring and summer of my junior year studying in Spain. Seeing a different side of life—a side I'd never been exposed to before—gave me a new sense of perspective and taught me not to take so much for granted. When I got back, I knew I wanted to keep learning Spanish—to become fluent to the level of a native speaker, and to do something to help people along the way, if I could.... I had always thought about joining the Peace Corps, but I was never sure I could actually do it...

By my senior year, the more I thought about all the things I'd done, the more I knew that this time, I was strong enough to handle an experience like the Peace Corps. The hardest parts of my life have made me feel the most whole and the proudest of myself. I guess I needed to beat cancer to find out that I can do anything.

Directions: Answer the following questions about the article "Survivor."

1. The subject of "Survivor" was diagnosed with
   A. cancer of the blood (leukemia)
   B. cancer of the thyroid
   C. cancer of the throat
   D. hyperthyroidism
   E. none of the above

2. The thyroid works to regulate your metabolism or
   A. speed of body processes
   B. growth over a lifetime
   C. organ functions
   D. fighting off of disease
   E. none of the above

3. A *biopsy* is
   A. a gland in your neck
   B. a complete physical exam
   C. a procedure to extract blood or tissue from the body for analysis
   D. a drug that regulates your hormones
   E. a needle

4. Some of the symptoms of hypothyroidism are
   A. low energy
   B. depression or sadness
   C. sleeplessness
   D. A and B
   E. A and C

5. Thyroid replacement hormones
   A. cause hormonal imbalance
   B. are called Synthroid
   C. make you feel tired
   D. are effective right away
   E. simulate the way the thyroid works

6. Describe the events in Bess's life leading up to her decision to go into the Peace Corps.

7. Describe how Bess's battle with cancer affected her physically and emotionally. How was her academic and social life affected?

8. How did Bess feel about her experience with cancer?

Booster Lesson 8

9. Write an essay describing an experience in which you, someone you know, or a person or character you have read about was a "survivor." What was the experience? How did you or that person or character handle the experience? What were its impacts? What did the experience teach you (or the person or character)?

10. The Peace Corps is a government agency that sends volunteers to developing countries to assist communities in setting up businesses, to teach English, to train health care workers, to plant trees, and to do many other activities depending on the needs of the host country.

Write a letter of application to join the Peace Corps as if you were Bess Judson of "Survivor." Describe why you are a good candidate and the reasons they should accept your application.

QAR Reflections Journal

_____
_____
_____
_____
_____

QAR Reflections Journal

QAR Reflections Journal

SUPER QAR™

for Test-Wise Students

Student Activity Book

This book belongs to:

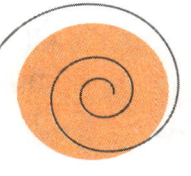

_____

Wright Group

The McGraw·Hill Companies

Question Answer Relationships

In the Book

Right There

The answer is "right there" in the text. It is often a detail question.

Think and Search

The answer is in the text and involves cross-text searches. Identifying text structures such as the following helps organize your answer.

- Simple List
- Explanation
- Sequence
- Compare and Contrast
- Cause and Effect
- Problem and Solution

In My Head

Author and Me

The information to answer the question comes from background knowledge. You need to read the text and understand the question and you need to make connections.

- Text to Self: How the text affects the way you think or believe.
- Text to Text: Make connections with different texts you've read.
- Text to Themes: Use what you've read to generalize, identify themes, or interpret text.

On My Own

All the ideas and information to answer the question come from background knowledge, experiences, and beliefs. The question can be answered without reading the text.

Directions: Read this passage from *American History: The Early Years to 1877* by Donald A. Ritchie and Albert S. Broussard.

The Women's Rights Movement

Women took a special interest in the antislavery movement. As they fought for social reform for African Americans, they realized that they also lacked full social and political rights. When women tried to participate in the antislavery movement, they often met resistance. As a result, many abolitionists became crusaders for women's rights.

Equal rights for women would require major reform. In the 1800s women actually had fewer rights than in colonial times. They had few political or legal rights. Women could not vote or hold public office. A woman's husband owned all of her property.

Women from New England to Ohio joined the antislavery societies. Many saw similarities between the treatment of enslaved persons and women.

Journalist Margaret Fuller observed that "there exists in the minds of men a tone of feeling toward women as towards slaves." Abolitionists Angelina and Sarah Grimké confronted this feeling when they spoke to antislavery groups. Audiences did not criticize their stand on slavery. They did, though, question their right to speak in public.

As a result, the Grimkés soon found themselves in the midst of "an entirely new contest—a contest for the rights of woman." Sarah wrote that "all I ask… is that [men] will take their feet from off our necks and permit us to stand upright."

QAR Characteristics

IN THE BOOK

Right There

Source:

The answer is found in the text.

The answer is easily found within a single statement or paragraph.

Wording:

The wording of the question is found in the text and may be repeated in the answer.

The answer may use the exact wording in the text.

Content:

The answer is usually a definition, a fact, or a detail from the text.

Format:

The question-answer format is usually multiple-choice.

Think and Search

Source:

The answer is found in the text.

The answer is found in more than one statement, paragraph, or section of the text.

Wording:

The wording of the question may or may not be found in the text.

The answer may or may not use the wording in the text.

Content:

The answer may require inferring or summarizing from information given in the text.

The answer may address the main idea of the text.

Format:

The question-answer format may be multiple-choice or short answer.

IN MY HEAD

Author and Me

Source:

The answer is based on my own knowledge and experience.

The answer combines an understanding of the text with my own knowledge or experience. It may connect to other texts I have read.

Wording:

The wording of the question is unlikely to be found in the text.

The answer may or may not use wording in the text. The answer may refer to or draw on points made in the text.

Content:

The answer is a narrative inferred from or based on information given in the text.

The answer addresses the main idea or theme of the text.

Format:

The question-answer format may be multiple-choice, short answer, or extended response (essay).

On My Own

Source:

The answer is based on my own knowledge and experience.

The answer is independent of the text. It is related to the general topic of the text but comes from my own experience, knowledge, and reading.

Wording:

The wording of the question is not found in the text.

The answer will not use wording in the text.

Content:

The answer is a personal narrative (explanation, opinion, description) related to the general topic or theme of the text.

Format:

The question-answer format is usually short answer or extended response (essay).

Concept Lesson 1   5

Directions: Reread the passage on page 3. Answer the questions and identify the QAR. On the next page, write the strategies you used to find the answers.

QUESTION / ANSWER / QAR

1. What did audiences of the antislavery speakers criticize?

   QAR: _____

2. What were some rights women lacked in the 1800s?

   QAR: _____

3. In this passage, the term *abolitionists* refers to what?

   QAR: _____

4. What is our society's attitude toward women's rights today?

   QAR: _____

STRATEGY

1.

2.

3.

4.

Directions: Write a short-answer question about the text on page 3 for each type of QAR. Then tell why the question represents that QAR.

Right There

Question	Answer	Why this is a Right There QAR

Think and Search

Question	Answer	Why this is a Think and Search QAR

Author and Me

Question	Answer	Why this is an Author and Me QAR

On My Own

Question	Answer	Why this is an On My Own QAR

Concept Lesson 1

Directions: Write four new questions about the text on page 3 in the spaces provided. (Do not fill in the answers.) When instructed to do so, exchange your *Student Activity Book* with a partner and answer each other's questions.

Partner's Name: _____

Directions: Answer each question, identify the QAR, and explain how you know what kind of QAR it is.

1.

   Answer:

   QAR:

   How do you know:

2.

   Answer:

   QAR:

   How do you know:

Concept Lesson 1

3.

Answer:

QAR:

How do you know:

4.

Answer:

QAR:

How do you know:

Directions: Read this passage from *Sue at the Field Museum*.

Sue the T-Rex

The first *T. rex* specimen was found in 1900. Since then, only seven skeletons that are more than half complete have been discovered. Of these, Sue is the largest, most complete, and best preserved *T. rex* ever found. Most of Sue's bones are in excellent condition and have a high degree of surface detail. Sixty-seven million years after her death, it is still possible to see fine details showing where muscles, tendons, and other soft tissues rested against or attached to the bone. Sue's completeness, combined with the exquisite preservation of the bones, makes her an invaluable scientific resource, permitting highly detailed study of *T. rex* anatomy.

In the summer of 1990, Sue Hendrickson was working as a fossil hunter with a commercial fossil-collecting team near Faith, South Dakota. On August 12 most of the team went into town to get a flat tire fixed and to take a short break from the heat. Sue stayed behind to look for fossils. She hiked over to some sandstone bluffs that had previously caught her attention. Within minutes she spotted some bone fragments on the ground. She scanned the cliffs above to find out where the fragments had fallen from and saw dinosaur bones—big ones. She climbed up the cliff for a better look at the bones, and saw they were huge. She thought she had found a *T. rex*, and when the team returned, they confirmed her find and promptly named it "Sue" in her honor.

Soon after Sue was discovered, her bones became the center of a dispute. Who owned the fossil?

To dig up dinosaurs, you always need the landowner's permission. But in Sue's case it was unclear whose land it was because . . . the bones were found on land that was part of a Sioux Indian reservation, BUT . . . the land belonged to a private rancher, BUT . . . the rancher was part Sioux, and his land was held in trust by the U.S. government. While people argued about who owned Sue, the bones were safely locked away in storerooms at the South Dakota School of Mines and Technology. In the end, a judge decided that Sue was held in trust by the U.S. government for the rancher on whose property the skeleton had been found. The rancher, in turn, decided to sell Sue at public auction.

Following the long custody battle, Sue was sold at Sotheby's auction house in New York on October 4, 1997. Just eight minutes after the bidding started, the Field Museum of Chicago purchased Sue for nearly $8.4 million—the most money ever paid for a fossil. On May 17, 2000, the Field Museum unveiled Sue, the largest, most complete, and best preserved *T. rex* fossil yet discovered.

Directions: Answer the questions below about the text on page 11. Then, identify the text structure and the strategy you used to find the answer.

QUESTION / ANSWER

1. Who found Sue?
   - **A.** A rancher
   - **B.** A hike
   - **C.** A professional fossil hunter
   - **D.** None of the above

2. What happened after Sue was found?
   - **A.** The ownership of the bones was contested.
   - **B.** The bones were temporarily stored at a university.
   - **C.** The bones were put on display at a museum.
   - **D.** All of the above.

3. Why was the ownership of the bones unclear?

4. Why was Sue an important find?

TEXT STRUCTURE	STRATEGY
1.	1.
2.	2.
3.	3.
4.	4.

Concept Lesson 2

Directions: Write two short-answer Think and Search questions about the text on page 11. Then for each question, write the answer, identify the text structure, and tell why the QAR is Think and Search.

1.

   Answer:

   Text Structure:

   Why this is a Think and Search QAR:

2.

   Answer:

   Text Structure:

   Why this is a Think and Search QAR:

Directions: Write two new questions about the text on page 11 in the spaces provided. (Do not fill in the answers.) When instructed to do so, exchange your *Student Activity Book* with a partner and answer each other's questions.

Partner's Name: _____

Directions: Answer each question, identify the QAR, explain how you know what kind of QAR it is, and identify the strategies you used.

1.

   Answer:

   QAR:

   How do you know:

   Strategies for finding the answer:

2.

   Answer:

   QAR:

   How do you know:

   Strategies for finding the answer:

Concept Lesson 2   15

In My Head Sample Questions

1. **Author and Me: Text to Self**
   - How would you feel if you were the main character?
   - Compare your experience with that of someone in the story.
   - How does the situation today reflect the outcome of events described in the text?

   Notes:

2. **Author and Me: Text to Text**
   - Compare the main character with a character in another text you have read. How is he or she the same or different?

   Notes:

3. **Author and Me: Text to Themes**
   - What is the theme of the story?
   - What do you think was the author's primary message to the reader?

   Notes:

4. **On My Own**
   - Do you think women have full civil rights? Why or why not? Explain your conclusion.
   - Describe a time when you were scared. Why were you frightened? What happened?

   Notes:

Directions: Read this excerpt from *The Red Badge of Courage: An Episode of the American Civil War* by Stephen Crane. Then answer the questions on the next page.

The Red Badge of Courage

The cold passed reluctantly from the earth, and the retiring fogs revealed an army stretched out on the hills, resting. As the landscape changed from brown to green, the army awakened, and began to tremble with eagerness at the noise of rumors....

Once a certain tall soldier developed virtues and went resolutely to wash a shirt. He came flying back from a brook waving his garment bannerlike. He was swelled with a tale he had heard from a reliable friend, who had heard it from a truthful cavalryman, who had heard it from his trustworthy brother, one of the orderlies at division headquarters. He adopted the important air of a herald in red and gold. "We're goin' t' move t' morrah—sure," he said pompously to a group in the company street. "We're goin' 'way up the river, cut across, an' come around in behint 'em."

To his attentive audience he drew a loud and elaborate plan of a very brilliant campaign. When he had finished, the blue-clothed men scattered into small arguing groups between the rows of squat brown huts.... "It's a lie! that's all it is—a thunderin' lie!" said another private loudly. His smooth face was flushed, and his hands were thrust sulkily into his trousers' pockets. He took the matter as an affront to him. "I don't believe the derned old army's ever going to move. We're set. I've got ready to move eight times in the last two weeks, and we ain't moved yet."

The tall soldier felt called upon to defend the truth of a rumor he himself had introduced. He and the loud one came near to fighting over it....

Many of the men engaged in a spirited debate. One outlined in a peculiarly lucid manner all the plans of the commanding general. He was opposed by men who advocated that there were other plans of campaign. They clamored at each other, numbers making futile bids for the popular attention. Meanwhile, the soldier who had fetched the rumor bustled about with much importance....

There was a youthful private who listened with eager ears to the words of the tall soldier and to the varied comments of his comrades. After receiving a fill of discussions concerning marches and attacks, he went to his hut and crawled through an intricate hole that served it as a door. He wished to be alone with some new thoughts that had lately come to him....

The youth was in a little trance of astonishment. So they were at last going to fight. On the morrow, perhaps, there would be a battle, and he would be in it. For a time he was obliged to labor to make himself believe. He could not accept with assurance an omen that he was about to mingle in one of those great affairs of the earth.

He had, of course, dreamed of battles all his life—of vague and bloody conflicts that had thrilled him with their sweep and fire. In visions he had seen himself in many struggles. He had imagined peoples secure in the shadow of his eagle-eyed prowess. But awake he had regarded battles as crimson blotches on the pages of the past. He had put them as things of the bygone with his thought-images of heavy crowns and high castles. There was a portion of the world's history which he had regarded as the time of wars, but it, he thought, had been long gone over the horizon and had disappeared forever.

Directions: Answer the following questions about the text on page 17. Indicate the type of QAR, where you found the answer, and the strategies you used to find the answer.

QUESTION / ANSWER / QAR

1. Describe how the soldiers responded to the rumor of battle and how you react to rumors or gossip that you hear.

   QAR: _____

2. The "youth" in this passage "was about to mingle in one of those great affairs of the earth." Compare this "great affair" with an event in another story you have read.

   QAR: _____

3. In this passage, one of the author's themes is

   A. how the uncertainty of war affected the soldiers
   B. people will believe anything they hear
   C. the soldiers were not afraid to die
   D. the virtues of bravery

   QAR: _____

4. What would it be like to be a soldier facing battle? What would your thoughts and concerns be?

   QAR: _____

Concept Lesson 3

SOURCE	STRATEGY
1.	1.
2.	2.
3.	3.
4.	4.

Concept Lesson 3

Directions: Write two short-answer In My Head questions about the text on page 17. Then write the answers and why the QAR categories are In My Head.

Question	Answer	Why this is an In My Head QAR

Question	Answer	Why this is an In My Head QAR

Concept Lesson 3

Directions: Write two new questions about the text on page 17 in the spaces provided. (Do not fill in the answers.) When instructed to do so, exchange your *Student Activity Book* with a partner and answer each other's questions.

Partner's Name: _____

Directions: Answer each question, identify the QAR, and explain how you know what type of QAR it is.

1.

   Answer:

   QAR:

   How do you know:

2.

   Answer:

   QAR:

   How do you know:

Concept Lesson 3

Test-Taking Strategies

Before you read the text...
- Read the test questions first.
- Scan for key words in the text.
- Skim first and last sentences; read the text quickly to find the main idea.

As you read...
- Circle, underline, or highlight key words or phrases.
- Identify important information and make notes.
- Predict what will happen next.
- Connect to the text. Ask yourself: What do I already know about this topic? What else have I read about this topic? Have I experienced something similar?
- Identify the theme.

Before you answer the question...
- Reread the question.
- Identify the QAR.
- Reread or skim the text.
- Scan your notes and words or phrases that you highlighted in the text.
- Brainstorm an answer and briefly note your thoughts. For an essay question, make a short outline of your answer.

For your answer...
- Summarize, infer, draw conclusions, or make connections.
- Support your answer with details from the text.
- Write complete sentences. Use conventional grammar, punctuation, and spelling.
- Pace yourself. Don't spend too much time on any one answer.

Directions: Read the following excerpt from *Ellen Foster* by Kaye Gibbons.

Chapter 1, Part 1

When I was little I would think of ways to kill my daddy…

He drank his own self to death the year after the County moved me out… And I can say for a fact that I am better off now than when he was alive.

I live in a clean brick house and mostly I am left to myself. When I start to carry an odor I take a bath and folks tell me how sweet I look.

There is a plenty to eat here and if we run out of something we just go to the store and get some more. I had me a egg sandwich for breakfast, mayonnaise on both sides. And I may fix me another one for lunch.

Two years ago I did not have much of anything. Not that I live in the lap of luxury now but I am proud for the schoolbus to pick me up here every morning. My stylish well-groomed self standing in the front yard with the grass green and the hedge bushes square.

I figure I made out pretty good considering the rest of my family is either dead or crazy…

Oh but I do remember when I was scared. Everything was so wrong like somebody had knocked something loose and my family was shaking itself to death. Some wild ride broke and the one in charge strolled off and let us spin and shake and fly off the rail. And they both died tired of the wild crazy spinning and wore out and sick…

Even my mama's skin looked tired of holding in her weak self. She would prop herself up by the refrigerator and watch my daddy go round the table swearing at all who did him wrong. She looked all sad in her face like it was all her fault.

She comes home from the hospital sometimes. If I was her I would stay there. All laid up in the air conditioning with folks patting your head and bringing you fruit baskets.

Oh no. She comes in and he lets into her right away. Carrying on. Set up in his E-Z lounger like he is King for a Day. You bring me this or that he might say.

She comes in the door and he asks about supper right off. What does she have planned? he wants to know. Wouldn't he like to know what I myself have planned?… More like a big mean baby than a grown man…

Big wind-up toy of a man. He is just too sorry to talk back to even if he is my daddy. And she is too limp and too sore to get up the breath to push the words out to stop it all. She just stands there and lets him work out his evil on her.

Get in the kitchen and fix me something to eat. I had to cook the whole time you was gone, he tells her.

And that was some lie he made up. Cook for his own self. Ha. If I did not feed us both we had to go into town and get take-out chicken. I myself was looking forward to something fit to eat but I was not about to say anything.

Directions: Complete this chart as you work together with your peers and teacher.

QUESTION / ANSWER / QAR

1. The relationship Ellen had with her dad was that
   A. he took care of her
   B. she took care of him
   C. she lived away from him
   D. she admired him

   QAR: _____

2. What has happened to Ellen in the past two years?

   QAR: _____

3. Compare Ellen's old life with her new life.

   QAR: _____

4. What does Ellen value most in life?

   QAR: _____

STRATEGY

1.

2.

3.

4.

Directions: Read more from *Ellen Foster*. Then answer the questions on pages 27 through 29.

Chapter 1, Part 2

Nobody yells after anybody to do this or that here.

My new mama lays out the food and we all take a turn to dish it out. Then we eat and have a good time. Toast or biscuits with anything you please. Eggs any style. Corn cut off the cob the same day we eat it. I keep my elbows off the table and wipe my mouth like a lady. …When everybody is done eating my new mama puts the dishes in a thing, shuts the door, cuts on it, and Wa-La they are clean

My mama does not say a word about being tired or sore. She did ask who kept everything so clean and he took the credit. I do not know who he thinks he fooled. I knew he lied and my mama did too. She just asked to be saying something.

Mama puts the food out on the table and he wants to know what I am staring at. At you humped over your plate like one of us is about to snatch it from you. You old hog. But I do not say it.

Why don't you eat? he wants to know.

I don't have an appetite, I say back.

Well, you better eat. Your mama looks like this might be her last supper.

He is so sure he's funny that he laughs at his own self…

Now at my new mama's I lay up late in the day and watch the rain fall outside. Not one thing is pressing on me to get done here.

I have a bag of candy to eat on. One piece at a time. Make it last. All I got left to do is eat supper and wash myself.

Look around my room. It is so nice.

When I accumulate enough money I plan to get some colored glass things that you dangle from the window glass. I lay here and feature how that would look. I already got pink checkerboard curtains with dingleballs around the edges. My new mama sewed them for me. She also sewed matching sacks that I cram my pillows into every morning.

Everything matches. It is all so neat and clean…

The yelling makes my mama jump and if she was asleep she is awake now. Grits her teeth every time he calls out damn this or that. The more he drinks the less sense he makes.

By the time the dog races come on he's stretched out on the bathroom floor and can't get up. I know I need to go in there and poke him. Same thing every Saturday…

I get up and go in there and tell him to get up that folks got to come in here and do their business.

He can go lay in the truck.

He just grunts and grabs at my ankle and misses.

Get on up I say again to him. You got to be firm when he is like this. He'd lay there and rot if I let him so I nudge him with my foot. I will not touch my hands to him. Makes me want to heave my own self seeing him pull himself up on the sink. He zig-zags out through the living room and

Chapter 1, Part 2 (continued)

I guess he makes it out the door. I don't hear him fall down the steps.

And where did she come from? Standing in the door looking at it all.

Get back in bed, I say to mama.

Mama's easy to tend to. She goes back in the bedroom. Not a bit of trouble. Just stiff and hard to move around. I get her back in the bed and tell her he's outside for the night. She starts to whimper and I say it is no reason to cry. But she will wear herself out crying.

I ought to lock him out.

A grown man that should be bringing her food to nibble on and books to look at. No but he is taking care of his own self tonight. Just like she is not sick or kin to him.

A storm is coming up. And I will lay here with my mama until I see her chest rise up and sink down regular. Deep and regular and far away from the man in the truck.

Directions: Answer the questions below and on the next two pages. Identify the QAR categories and the test-taking strategies you used.

1. Ellen is most upset that her father

    A. doesn't work

    B. abuses her mother

    C. does not take care of her mother

    D. does not take care of her

    QAR: _____

    Test-Taking Strategy:

2. Describe Ellen's feelings toward her father during the scene when her mother has returned home.

    QAR: _____
    Test-Taking Strategy:

Concept Lesson 4

3. What role has Ellen taken on in her birth family and why?

    QAR: _____
    Test-Taking Strategy:

4. Ellen's feelings toward her father could best be described as
    A. anger
    B. pity
    C. disgust
    D. A and B
    E. A and C
    QAR: _____
    Test-Taking Strategy:

5. Describe the stability and simple pleasures of Ellen's new life.

    QAR: _____
    Test-Taking Strategy:

6. If Ellen went to your school, what would you think of her? Give specific examples and reasons.

    QAR: _____
    Test-Taking Strategy:

7. Ellen's new life is like her old one because
   A. no one yells
   B. her mother takes care of her
   C. she has plenty to eat
   D. she lives in a messy place
   E. none of the above

   QAR: _____
   Test-Taking Strategy:

8. How does Ellen's birth mother react to her husband?

   QAR: _____
   Test-Taking Strategy:

9. Compare and contrast Ellen's new life with her old life. Use details from the story to support your answer.

   QAR: _____
   Test-Taking Strategy:

10. Ellen had to struggle to survive in her birth family. Describe a personal experience in which you struggled for success, happiness, stability, approval, or some other goal.

    QAR: _____
    Test-Taking Strategy:

Concept Lesson 4

Directions: Read the following article by Marcella J. Kehus.

The Complexities of Cloning

Before 1996, few people had actually considered cloning a real possibility beyond something you might read about or see in a science fiction movie. But in July of that year, when Dolly the ewe (baby sheep) was born as a clone of her mother, some great debates began that are still raging in many areas. Cloning, or the creating of a living replica from DNA from a body cell, took quite a long time to develop before it actually worked with Dolly as its first success. Now people from politicians to religious leaders to scientists and the general public continue to argue over whether this technology should be applied to humans. The basic debate comes down to: Should we or should we not allow the cloning of human beings? And, if we do so, what are the possible results?

Now that the procedure for cloning has been discovered, it seems only a matter of time before it is applied to humans. This is where a number of people, specialists and general citizens alike, have serious concerns. One of their primary concerns, which often comes up with every new technology, are the number of ways that such a technology might be abused. For example, what if a certain group wanted to use cloning to create an army of exact duplicate soldiers or creatures to carry out their evil deeds? And, because cloning can include genetic engineering, or selecting just the right genes to create a certain kind of being (strong, green eyes, etc.), the idea of creating a look-alike super-human race reminds people quickly of the terrible possibilities of Hitler-like beliefs if given the power of cloning.

There are lesser kinds of abuses that the power of human cloning could inspire. Perhaps a former football player got his career cut short due to an injury; what would keep him from creating a clone of himself to play and become the star he always wanted to be? Cloning could become a fashionable way for other conceited people to just re-create themselves and the result may be a child who is never given a chance to become an individual.

On the other hand, there are impressive possibilities when it comes to human cloning. First, cloning is another possible solution for couples who are otherwise unable to have children of their own. In fact, the medical solutions made possible by clones are numerous including the supplying of life-saving transplant organs or bone marrow by cloned family members that would automatically match. And, when coupled with genetic engineering, cloning may allow us to create better humans as we discover more and more about disease and aging and produce clones who are better-equipped to survive.

Certainly, the possibilities of human cloning are scientifically possible. Yet, as with other new developments, one must carefully consider the possible outcomes—both good and bad. Ultimately, we as a society will make the decision as to whether human cloning's benefits outweigh its possible abuses and where we go from here.

Directions: Answer the following questions about the article on page 30 and identify each QAR.

1. According to the article, what "great debate" started in 1996?

   QAR: _____

2. What are other arguments against cloning that are not mentioned in the article?

   QAR: _____

3. Who is involved in the debate about human cloning?

   QAR: _____

4. What do you think is the strongest reason given for human cloning? Why?

   QAR: _____

5. What do you think is the strongest reason against human cloning? Why?

   QAR: _____

6. What are three different ways that individuals might benefit from human cloning?

   QAR: _____

7. Who do you think will make the final decision about whether or not human cloning is allowed?

   QAR: _____

Essay-Writing Tips, Part 1

- Before you start writing, identify the QAR.

- Create a short outline of your main thesis or idea and two or three main points that support your thesis. If you're stuck, do some brainstorming.

- Restate the question as a thesis or opening line(s).

- Answer all parts of the question. Check off each part as you go.

- For each part of the answer, note the specific part in the text that supports it.

- Include an introduction, at least two body paragraphs, and a conclusion.

- Present your ideas in a logical way. What comes first, second, third? What is your conclusion?

- If you have time, reread your essay to correct spelling, punctuation, or grammatical errors.

Directions: Reread the passage on page 30. Then choose a side for or against human cloning and write an essay to convince your audience to believe as you do.

Directions: Read "The Bungee Lunge" on pages 36 and 37. As you read, write five during reading questions in the spaces below. Identify the QAR that each question represents.

1.

   QAR: _____

2.

   QAR: _____

3.

   QAR: _____

4.

   QAR: _____

5.

   QAR: _____

Booster Lesson 1

Directions: Read this article by Karen McNulty.

The Bungee Lunge

Here's your giant rubber band. Now jump! It's only a 10-story plunge—and science will spring you back.

The Science Behind the Bounce

Ready?

When standing high on a jump platform, you have lots of potential (stored) energy.

Jump!

Leap off and your potential energy is converted to kinetic energy, the energy of motion. For a few seconds, you experience free fall, until there's no more slack in the cord.

Stret – t – ch

Then the cord starts to stretch. This stores the energy of your fall in the cord.

Bounce

This stored energy springs you back up. You fall and bounce again… and again…

Phew!

Each bounce disperses some of your energy, so eventually you stop. You'll have to hang around until someone lowers you to a raft or the ground.

You're hanging onto the railing of a bridge, 46 m above the river. Your friends on the bank below seem awfully small; looking at them makes you dizzy. Someone standing behind you is counting down "Three…two…one!" Defying every sane notion in your brain, you leap—headfirst.

The 100 km/h fall toward the water terrifies you. But just as you close your eyes for the icy plunge, something happens: You bounce back!

Better thank your lucky *bungee cord*—that wrist-thick band of latex rubber strapped to your ankles and anchored to the bridge. Because it was the right length, it kept you high and dry. And because it stret-t-t-ched and recoiled—giving you a few good bounces—it used up the energy of your fall so you didn't get torn limb from limb. Phew!

Those who have done it say it's the thrill of a lifetime—"a natural high." Others call it crazy. But everyone knows it as "bungee jumping," the sport springing up (and down) across the nation.

At least one group of people has been "bungee jumping" for ages: the men of Pentecost Island in the South Pacific. They make cords from elastic vines, lash them to their ankles, and plunge off wooden towers into pits of softened earth. For these islanders, jumping is a springtime ritual, meant to demonstrate courage and supposedly ensure a plentiful yam harvest.

In North America, jumpers take the bungee plunge just for the excitement of it. Scott Bergman, who runs a bungee-jumping company in California, explains the appeal. "It's a feeling of having absolutely no control—and loving it."

And it doesn't take any skill. Just $75 to $100 and *faith*—in physics. It's a simple physics equation, after all, that let's "jump masters" like Bergman determine how far the cord will stretch when you take the plunge—whether it will stretch too far.

The Bungee Lunge (continued)

Weighing the Odds

The major variables are the stretchiness, or *elasticity*, of the cord—predetermined by the manufacturer—and the jumper's weight. As you might guess, "the heavier you are, the more the cord is going to stretch," says physicist Peter Brancazio.

By weighing customers (they don't just ask), using the equation, and adjusting cords, jump masters have bounced thousands to safety. (There have been some deaths—usually caused by frayed cords or other faulty equipment.)

Jump experts can even adjust the cords to give their clients custom-made thrills. "When we jump off bridges in California," says Bergman, "we ask the people if they want to just touch the water, dunk their heads in, or go all the way. We can really get it that exact."

Really? "I wouldn't trust them," says Brancazio, "but I guess they can."

If, for example, Bergman calculates that you'll crack your skull on a rock in the river, he can shorten your cord. "That starts the stretch at a higher point off the ground," says Brancazio.

Or you can jump with two cords. "In that case," says Brancazio, your weight is "equally divided between the cords so each stretches half as far."

Chances are, you'll scream just as hard with fear and delight.

Directions: Write a short answer to the following questions based on the article on pages 36 and 37 and identify the QAR for each.

1. Explain how energy is stored and released in a bungee cord.

   QAR: _____

2. Summarize the points of view of the two experts (Scott Bergman and Peter Brancazio) quoted in the article. Why might they have different perspectives on bungee jumping?

   QAR: _____

3. Would you ever consider bungee jumping? What would be your major considerations in making a decision?

   QAR: _____

4. Compare bungee jumping in the South Pacific to California.

   QAR: _____

5. Compare the during reading questions you wrote on page 35 with the questions above. What types of QAR categories are there? Which of your questions prepared you for the questions asked above, if any?

   QAR: _____

Tips for Using Textbooks

Look at text features:

- Headings and subheadings
- Summaries (main idea, key points)
- Terms and their definitions
- Words bolded or highlighted in the text
- Captions for illustrations

Use previewing techniques:

- Preview comprehension questions or exercises at the end.
- Skim the first and last sentences of each paragraph.

Take notes and ask questions:

- Restate definitions and explanations in your own words.
- Connect to the text: What do I already know? What do I want to learn?
- Restate or paraphrase questions in your own words.

Directions: Read this passage from *American History: The Early Years to 1877*.

The Women's Rights Movement

Guide to Reading

Main Idea
Emboldened by their work in the antislavery movement, many women fought to improve their own status in society.

Read to Learn...
* why women became unhappy with their positions in the mid-1800s
* how working in the antislavery movement prepared women to fight for their own rights
* what arguments opponents used against the women's rights movement

Terms to Know
* abolitionist
* suffrage

Women took a special interest in the antislavery movement. As they fought for social reform for African Americans, they realized that they also lacked full social and political rights. When women such as Angelina and Sarah Grimké tried to participate actively in the antislavery movement, they often met resistance. As a result, many abolitionists became crusaders for women's rights.

Equal rights for women would require major reform. In the 1800s women actually had fewer rights than in colonial times. They had few political or legal rights. Women could not vote. They could not hold public office. A woman's husband owned all her property.

Antislavery Movement Gives Women a Boost

Women from New England to Ohio joined the antislavery societies. They worked hard, gathering signatures on thousands of petitions to send to Congress. They also read about and discussed the abuses of slavery. Many saw similarities between the treatment of enslaved persons and women.

In her book *Woman in the Nineteenth Century,* journalist **Margaret Fuller** observed that "there exists in the minds of men a tone of feeling toward women as towards slaves." Abolitionists Angelina and Sarah Grimké confronted this feeling when they spoke to antislavery groups. Audiences did not criticize their stand on slavery. They did, though, question their right to speak in public.

As a result, the Grimkés soon found themselves in the midst of "an entirely new contest—a contest for the rights of woman." Sarah wrote that "all I ask... is that [men] will take their feet from off our necks and permit us to stand upright."

The Women's Rights Movement

Their involvement in the antislavery movement and other reform movements gave women roles outside their homes and families. They learned valuable skills, such as organizing, working

The Women's Rights Movement (continued)

together, and speaking in public. Eventually they used these skills to further their own cause—the women's rights movement.

In 1840 nine women from the United States attended the World Anti-Slavery Convention in **London**. When the women arrived at the convention, however, the male delegates barred them from participating. The women and some male allies protested. On the first day of the convention, delegates debated the situation.

Clergy at the convention considered it improper for women to participate. Other male delegates declared women "unfit for public or business meetings." In the end, the majority of delegates decided that women could not take part in discussions. Instead, the women delegates would have to sit in the gallery behind a curtain.

Humiliated and angry, two of the women, Lucretia Coffin Mott and Elizabeth Cady Stanton, spent hours after the meetings talking about women's position in society. They realized that they could not bring about social change if they themselves lacked social and political rights. Stanton and Mott "resolved to hold a convention as soon as we returned home, and form a society to advocate the rights of women."

The Seneca Falls Convention

Eight years passed before the two friends organized their convention. On July 19, 1848, the first women's rights convention opened in Seneca Falls, New York. Both male and female delegates attended the convention. The delegates issued the Seneca Falls Declaration, which proclaimed that "all men and women are created equal."

Then the declaration listed several resolutions. One of them demanded suffrage, or the right to vote, for women. Even supporters of women's rights hesitated to pass this bold demand. Mott exclaimed, "Oh, Lizzie, thou will make us ridiculous! We must go slowly." But Stanton refused to withdraw the resolution. After much heated debate, it passed by a narrow margin.

The Seneca Falls Convention marked the beginning of an organized women's rights movement. Following the convention, women did not achieve all of their demands. They did, however, overcome some obstacles. Many states passed laws permitting women to own their own property and keep their earnings. Many men and women, though, continued to oppose the movement. Most politicians ignored or acted hostile to the issue of women's rights.

The Women's Rights Movement (continued)

Assessment

Check for Understanding
1. Define suffrage.
2. Why did women become unhappy with their position in the mid-1800s? About what areas of their daily lives were they most concerned?

Critical Thinking
3. **Comparing and Contrasting.** Contrast the views of the men and women who opposed the women's rights movement with those who supported it.

4. **Identifying Relationships.** Re-create the diagram shown here, and list how women's work in the antislavery movement prepared them to fight for their own rights.

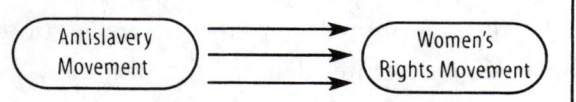

Antislavery Movement ⟶ Women's Rights Movement

Interdisciplinary Activity
5. **Citizenship.** Are women today denied any rights that men have? Draw up an agenda for a new Seneca Falls Convention listing topics for discussion.

Directions: Read "The Women's Rights Movement" on pages 40 and 41 and answer the questions from the Assessment section on page 42. Identify the type of QAR each question represents.

1.

   QAR: _____

2.

   QAR: _____

3.

   QAR: _____

4.

   QAR: _____

5.

   Write your agenda on a separate sheet or in your "QAR Reflections Journal."

   QAR: _____

Booster Lesson 2

Directions: Read this letter to President Franklin D. Roosevelt.

Dear Mr. President

Phila., Pa.
November 26, 1934

Honorable Franklin D. Roosevelt
Washington, D.C.

Dear Mr. President:

I am forced to write to you because we find ourselves in a very serious condition. For the last three or four years we have had depression and suffered with my family and little children severely. Now Since the Home Owners Loan Corporation opened up, I have been going up there in order to save my home, because there has been unemployment in my house for more than three years. You can imagine that I and my family have suffered from lack of water supply in my house for more than two years. Last winter I did not have coal and the pipes burst in my house and therefore could not make heat in the house. Now winter is here again and we are suffering of cold, no water in the house, and we are facing to be forced out of the house, because I have no money to move or pay so much money as they want when after making settlement. I am mother of little children, am sick and losing my health, and we are eight people in the family, and where can I go when I don't have money because no one is working in my house. The Home Loan Corporation wants $42. a month rent or else we will have to be on the street. I am living in this house for about ten years and when times were good we would put our last cent in the house and now I have no money, no home and no wheres to go. I beg of you to please help me and my family and little children for the sake of a sick mother and a suffering family to give this your immediate attention so we will not be forced to move or put out in the street.

Waiting and Hoping that you will act quickly.
Thanking you very much I remain

Mrs. E. L.

Directions: Read this excerpt from a speech by Robert Kennedy.

On the Death of Dr. Martin Luther King

This speech was given by Robert F. Kennedy on April 4, 1968, shortly after Dr. Martin Luther King, Jr. had been assassinated. At the time, Robert Kennedy was a U.S. Senator leading a race for the presidency, but he was assassinated a few months later.

Martin Luther King dedicated his life to love and to justice between fellow human beings. He died in the cause of that effort. In this difficult day, in this difficult time for the United States, it's perhaps well to ask what kind of a nation we are and what direction we want to move in.

For those of you who are black—considering the evidence evidently is that there were white people who were responsible—you can be filled with bitterness, and with hatred, and a desire for revenge.

We can move in that direction as a country, in greater polarization—black people amongst blacks, and white amongst whites, filled with hatred toward one another. Or we can make an effort, as Martin Luther King did, to understand and to comprehend, and replace that violence, that stain of bloodshed that has spread across our land, with an effort to understand, compassion and love.

For those of you who are black and are tempted to be filled with hatred and mistrust of the injustice of such an act, against all white people, I would only say that I can also feel in my own heart the same kind of feeling. I had a member of my family killed, but he was killed by a white man.

But we have to make an effort in the United States, we have to make an effort to understand, to get beyond these rather difficult times.

My favorite poet was Aeschylus. He once wrote: "Even in our sleep, pain which cannot forget falls drop by drop upon the heart, until, in our own despair, against our will, comes wisdom through the awful grace of God."

What we need in the United States is not division; what we need in the United States is not hatred; what we need in the United States is not violence and lawlessness, but is love and wisdom, and compassion toward one another, and a feeling of justice toward those who still suffer within our country, whether they be white or whether they be black.

So I ask you tonight to return home, to say a prayer for the family of Martin Luther King, yeah that's true, but more importantly to say a prayer for our own country, which all of us love—a prayer for understanding and that compassion of which I spoke. We can do well in this country. We will have difficult times. We've had difficult times in the past. And we will have difficult times in the future. It is not the end of violence; it is not the end of lawlessness; and it's not the end of disorder.

But the vast majority of white people and the vast majority of black people in this country want to live together, want to improve the quality of our life, and want justice for all human beings that abide in our land.

Let us dedicate ourselves to what the Greeks wrote so many years ago: to tame the savageness of man and make gentle the life of this world.

Let us dedicate ourselves to that, and say a prayer for our country and for our people.

Directions: Read pages 44 and 45 and then answer the following questions. Identify the QAR after your answer.

1. Compare and contrast the audience, purpose, and writing style of the two passages.

   QAR: _____

2. If you were President Roosevelt, how would you have responded to Mrs. E. L.'s letter? Why?

   QAR: _____

3. What would have been your reaction to Robert F. Kennedy's speech at the time. Why?

   QAR: _____

Best-Answer Strategies

IN THE BOOK

Right There
- Reread.
- Scan for key words.
- Recall key facts or figures.

Think and Search
- Reread.
- Scan for key words.
- Skim first and last sentences.
- Identify important information.
- Look for specific examples.
- Identify characters or people, events, plot, problem and solutions, etc.
- Identify the main idea or theme.
- Predict what will happen next.

IN MY HEAD

Author and Me
- Reread.
- Skim first and last sentences.
- Connect to important information What do I already know about this subject?
- Connect to the characters or people and events in the text.
- Connect to the main idea or theme.
- Predict what will happen next.
- Connect to other texts. What have I read before on this same subject or with this same theme?

On My Own
- Reread.
- Connect to the general theme or topic.
- Connect to other texts. What have I read before on this same subject or with this same theme?

Directions: Read this passage from *Lasers* by Lynne Kelly and answer the questions on page 49.

How a Laser Beam Is Made

The first pulse laser was made by Theodore H. Maiman of the United States in 1960. He used a ruby rod to make a short flash of laser light. The method has been improved since then, but the idea is the same.

1. A rod of ruby, about the size of a finger is used. Real ruby is very expensive, but synthetic ruby can be used.

2. The ends of the ruby rod are ground so they are perfectly smooth and parallel to each other. Each end is painted silver to make mirrors, but one end receives a thinner layer of paint than the other. This means that this end is only partially reflective.

3. A flash tube is wrapped around the ruby rob and connected to a battery. The flash tube and battery act as the power source.

4. When the flash tube is switched on, it produces bright, white light. This excites, or increases, the energy level of chromium atoms in the ruby. Light is reflected back and forth along the rod.

5. After a fraction of a second, a bright flash of red laser light will come out of the end of the ruby rod.

When the flash tube is switched on, chromium atoms in the ruby rod absorb some of the light energy. These atoms then give out energy again in the form of colored light. Light beams given out from one sort of atom that has been excited in this way will all be identical.

These identical light beams reflect back and forth along the ruby rod from one mirror to the other. As they do so, they excite more atoms, which give off more light. This goes on until the light beam has grown strong enough to break through the thinner mirror. All the light beams emitted from the thinner mirror will be identical and coherent and will travel in a straight line. They will be a laser beam.

The name *laser* comes from the way in which a laser beam is made. It is a form of light that is the result of many reflections between the mirrors on the ends of the ruby rod. This causes the energy to increase, or amplify. The chromium atoms that give off the pure light beam have been excited, or stimulated, by the flash of light. The atoms give out, or emit, pure monochromatic light, which is a form of electromagnetic radiation.

So a laser beam is the result of **L**ight **A**mplification by **S**timulated **E**mission of **R**adiation.

Directions: Answer the following questions about the text on page 48.

1. Which list includes the items used in generating laser light?
    A. ruby rod, flash tube, light switch
    B. synthetic ruby, mirrors, chromium atoms
    C. ruby rod, flash tube, battery
    D. ruby rod, reflective coating, flash tube, battery

2. What is the purpose of the mirrors at each end of the rod?
    A. They intensify the energy of the light beams as the light beams reflect back and forth between the mirrors.
    B. The protect the ends of the ruby rod as the high energy light beams travel back and forth.
    C. They decrease the level of energy of the chromium atoms in the ruby.
    D. None of the above.

3. What is the purpose of the flash tube and battery?
    A. They hold the ruby rod in place.
    B. They excite the chromium atoms.
    C. They make the light beams coherent.
    D. They generate the power needed to produce the energy for the laser beam.

4. How is a laser beam made?

5. Choose question 1, 2, or 3 above and analyze each response (A, B, C, D). Is it correct, partially correct, or incorrect? Why? Identify a statement or section of the passage that supports your answer.

Booster Lesson 4

The Road Not Taken

Two roads diverged in a yellow wood,
And sorry I could not travel both
And be one traveler, long I stood
And looked down one as far as I could
To where it bent in the undergrowth;

Then took the other, as just as fair,
And having perhaps the better claim,
Because it was grassy and wanted wear;
Though as for that the passing there
Had worn them really about the same,

And both that morning equally lay
In leaves no step had trodden black.
Oh, I kept the first for another day!
Yet knowing how way leads on to way,
I doubted if I should ever come back.

I shall be telling this with a sigh
Somewhere ages and ages hence:
Two roads diverged in a wood, and I—
I took the one less traveled by,
And that has made all the difference.

by Robert Frost

Life

They told me that Life could be just what I made it—
    Life could be fashioned and worn like a gown;
I, the designer; mine the decision
    Whether to wear it with bonnet or crown.

And so I selected the prettiest pattern—
    Life should be made of the rosiest hue—
Something unique, and a bit out of fashion,
    One that perhaps would be chosen by few.

But other folks came and they leaned o'er my shoulder;
    Somebody questioned the ultimate cost;
Somebody tangled the thread I was using;
    One day I found that my scissors were lost.

And somebody claimed the material faded;
    Somebody said I'd be tired ere 'twas worn;
Somebody's fingers, too pointed and spiteful,
    Snatched at the cloth, and I saw it was torn.

Oh! somebody tried to do all the sewing,
    Wanting always to advise or condone.
Here is my life, the product of many;
    Where is that gown I could fashion—alone?

by Nan Terrell Reed

Directions: This test has two parts. When you're finished with Part 1, go on to Part 2.

Part 1

Directions: Read the poems on page 50 and 51. Then write five Author and Me questions (connecting self to text, text to text, and text to theme) about the poems.

Author and Me Questions
for "The Road Not Taken"

1.

2.

3.

4.

5.

Author and Me Questions
for "Life"

1.

2.

3.

4.

5.

Booster Lesson 5

Part 2

Directions: Answer the following questions about the two poems. Support your answers with details from the text. Identify the QAR after each answer.

1. In "The Road Not Taken," how did the narrator know that one of the roads was "less traveled by"?

    QAR: _____

2. Why did the narrator choose "the road less traveled by"?

    QAR: _____

3. How does the narrator feel about his decision?

    QAR: _____

Booster Lesson 5

Part 2, continued

4. What is the main idea or theme of "The Road Not Taken"?

   QAR: _____

5. In the poem "Life," what does the author compare life to? What did she want her life to be like?

   QAR: _____

6. Who is the "Somebody" referred to in the poem? What does this somebody do?

   QAR: _____

7. At the end of "Life," how does the narrator feel about her life?

   QAR: _____

Part 2, continued

8. What is the main idea or theme of "Life"?

   QAR: _____

9. Compare and contrast the narrators of the poems "The Road Not Taken" and "Life." What were they seeking? How did they feel about their "road taken" and "gown" at the end?

   QAR: _____

10. Compare and contrast the main ideas or themes in each poem. How are they different? How are they similar?

    QAR: _____

Booster Lesson 5

Solving Math Story Problems

Ask yourself...

1. **What is given?**

   Identify the information already stated or given in the problem.

2. **What am I supposed to figure out?**

   Restate the problem in terms of the unknown quantity.

3. **What is the math concept?**

   Identify the math concept or concepts you have to know. What have you already learned about this concept?

Do the work...

4. **Set up the problem.**

   > Always show your work. If you get an incorrect answer because of a computation error, you may get partial credit for setting up the problem correctly and showing how you got the answer.

5. **Do the calculation.**

6. **Select or write your answer.**

Booster Lesson 6

Directions: Answer the following question. Refer to the steps on page 56 if necessary.

In Malia's eighth-grade class, 3 out of 5 students are girls. In a class of 30 students, how many are girls?

A. 12
B. 18
C. 20
D. 22

1. What is given?

2. What am I supposed to figure out?

3. What is the math concept?

4. Set up the problem.

5. Do the calculation.

6. Select or write your answer.

Booster Lesson 6

Essay-Writing Tips, Part 2

Purpose

Identify the purpose of the essay:

- Narration
- Information
- Persuasion

Audience

Identify who you are writing for.

Text Type

Identify the text type:

- Formal essay
- Letter
- Editorial
- Newspaper or journal article
- Procedure
- Others

Evaluation

- **Development:** Are the ideas well developed? Does the essay have good supporting or descriptive details?

- **Organization:** Is the essay well organized? Does it have good transitions between ideas and paragraphs?

- **Use of language:** Is the sentence structure varied? Is descriptive or figurative language used effectively?

- **Mechanics:** Do grammatical, spelling, and punctuation errors interfere with understanding the content?

Directions: Complete this worksheet as you work together with your peers and teacher.

ESSAY-WRITING WORKSHEET

Write an article for the school newspaper explaining the benefits of playing computer games.

QAR:

Purpose:

Audience:

Text Type:

Brainstorm Ideas:

Outline:

Directions: With a partner, complete the worksheet. Then write your letter on the next page.

ESSAY-WRITING WORKSHEET

Think of a social issue affecting your school, neighborhood, or community (for example, pollution, noise, litter, homelessness, traffic, etc.). Write a letter to a public official describing the problem and asking for help. Explain what you think should be done to solve it and why.

QAR:

Purpose:

Audience:

Text Type:

Brainstorm Ideas:

Outline:

Directions: Use this page to write your letter.

Directions: Complete this worksheet and write your essay on the next page.

ESSAY-WRITING WORKSHEET

Imagine that you just saw on the news that computer scientists have perfected the technologies behind artificial intelligence and expect manufacturers to begin making robots soon with many—but not all—human capabilities.

Explain what you and your family members would like robots to do if you could buy them. What kinds of things do you think the robots should or should not do?

QAR:

Purpose:

Audience:

Text Type:

Brainstorm Ideas:

Outline:

Booster Lesson 7

Directions: Use this page to write your essay.

Directions: Read the following article from *Teen Vogue,* as told to Sarah Brown by Bess Judson. Then answer the questions on pages 66 through 69.

Survivor

I noticed the bump during the summer. I thought it was cool the way it moved when I swallowed, like a seed sliding under the skin of an orange slice. I made my mom touch it. "Maybe it's a tumor!" I said, laughing. "It's probably just a swollen gland or something. We'll get it checked out if it doesn't go away soon," she said, and sent me off to school.

I was psyched to go to college... My first semester at Hamilton, in upstate New York, was so much fun. I joined the rugby team and started feeling really good about myself again.

I didn't even think about my bump until Christmas break, when I switched from a pediatrician to a general practitioner, who gave me a complete physical. As soon as she felt the lump on my thyroid she sent me for a needle biopsy. I thought it was routine, although I was surprised I went for tests right away, instead of having to schedule an appointment.

And then I went back to school. The first night I was back, my doctor called. The tumor was malignant. I had cancer, and in one week, I was scheduled to have an operation to remove my thyroid. I hung up the phone thinking back to the pink fluid the doctor had removed from my bump during the biopsy. The liquid had looked so harmless inside the syringe, like water used to clean a red paintbrush.

I was totally petrified. As soon as you hear that word—*cancer*—no one knows what to say. Doctors don't really even know that much about it. All they can do is try to cut it out.

My surgeon told me I'd need to take two weeks off from school, which is what I'd planned to do. I spent two nights in the hospital, in and out of sleep. Every few hours a man who called himself the Vampire would wake me up to draw my blood. When I finally stood up to walk, I had to hold my mother's arm to stay on my feet. I inched through the halls, rolling my IV beside me like a fish dragging the rod that hooked it....

Your thyroid is a gland in your neck—the part of your body that regulates metabolism (the physical and chemical processes that essentially maintain life). It also controls a lot of your hormones, and for about a month, I was just miserable. After surgery, I had to wait awhile before I could start taking thyroid-replacement hormones (which simulate the way an actual thyroid works), so my entire hormonal makeup was out of whack. I was tired and I was sad and I would cry all the time about nothing. I was what they call hypothyroid—I felt sluggish and just really crummy.

When I was finally allowed to start taking Synthroid (synthetic thyroid hormones), I was expecting to feel normal right away—to go back to classes and to play rugby in the spring. They have to raise the hormones to the right levels incrementally, so in the beginning, I was taking only about half the level I am now. I went back to school, and I did play rugby, but let's just say I wasn't a huge success. I was so much slower than I'd been before. My friends were totally supportive—they couldn't believe I was playing at all. I signed up for a full course load, but I ended up having to drop a class. In the fall semester, I'd gotten some C's and a D... but this time, somehow, I got straight A's. I think I was just happy to be back, happy I was able to pull through and rebound...

Survivor (continued)

I spent the spring and summer of my junior year studying in Spain. Seeing a different side of life—a side I'd never been exposed to before—gave me a new sense of perspective and taught me not to take so much for granted. When I got back, I knew I wanted to keep learning Spanish—to become fluent to the level of a native speaker, and to do something to help people along the way, if I could.... I had always thought about joining the Peace Corps, but I was never sure I could actually do it...

By my senior year, the more I thought about all the things I'd done, the more I knew that this time, I was strong enough to handle an experience like the Peace Corps. The hardest parts of my life have made me feel the most whole and the proudest of myself. I guess I needed to beat cancer to find out that I can do anything.

Booster Lesson 8

Directions: Answer the following questions about the article "Survivor."

1. The subject of "Survivor" was diagnosed with
   A. cancer of the blood (leukemia)
   B. cancer of the thyroid
   C. cancer of the throat
   D. hyperthyroidism
   E. none of the above

2. The thyroid works to regulate your metabolism or
   A. speed of body processes
   B. growth over a lifetime
   C. organ functions
   D. fighting off of disease
   E. none of the above

3. A *biopsy* is
   A. a gland in your neck
   B. a complete physical exam
   C. a procedure to extract blood or tissue from the body for analysis
   D. a drug that regulates your hormones
   E. a needle

4. Some of the symptoms of hypothyroidism are
   A. low energy
   B. depression or sadness
   C. sleeplessness
   D. A and B
   E. A and C

5. Thyroid replacement hormones
   A. cause hormonal imbalance
   B. are called Synthroid
   C. make you feel tired
   D. are effective right away
   E. simulate the way the thyroid works

6. Describe the events in Bess's life leading up to her decision to go into the Peace Corps.

7. Describe how Bess's battle with cancer affected her physically and emotionally. How was her academic and social life affected?

8. How did Bess feel about her experience with cancer?

9. Write an essay describing an experience in which you, someone you know, or a person or character you have read about was a "survivor." What was the experience? How did you or that person or character handle the experience? What were its impacts? What did the experience teach you (or the person or character)?

10. The Peace Corps is a government agency that sends volunteers to developing countries to assist communities in setting up businesses, to teach English, to train health care workers, to plant trees, and to do many other activities depending on the needs of the host country.

Write a letter of application to join the Peace Corps as if you were Bess Judson of "Survivor." Describe why you are a good candidate and the reasons they should accept your application.

QAR Reflections Journal

_____
_____
_____
_____
_____

QAR Reflections Journal

SUPER QAR™

for Test-Wise Students

Student Activity Book

This book belongs to:

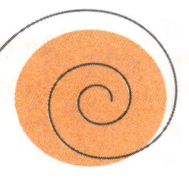

Wright Group

The McGraw·Hill Companies

Question Answer Relationships

In the Book

Right There

The answer is "right there" in the text. It is often a detail question.

Think and Search

The answer is in the text and involves cross-text searches. Identifying text structures such as the following helps organize your answer.

- Simple List
- Explanation
- Sequence
- Compare and Contrast
- Cause and Effect
- Problem and Solution

In My Head

Author and Me

The information to answer the question comes from background knowledge. You need to read the text and understand the question and you need to make connections.

- **Text to Self:** How the text affects the way you think or believe.
- **Text to Text:** Make connections with different texts you've read.
- **Text to Themes:** Use what you've read to generalize, identify themes, or interpret text.

On My Own

All the ideas and information to answer the question come from background knowledge, experiences, and beliefs. The question can be answered without reading the text.

Directions: Read this passage from *American History: The Early Years to 1877* by Donald A. Ritchie and Albert S. Broussard.

The Women's Rights Movement

Women took a special interest in the antislavery movement. As they fought for social reform for African Americans, they realized that they also lacked full social and political rights. When women tried to participate in the antislavery movement, they often met resistance. As a result, many abolitionists became crusaders for women's rights.

Equal rights for women would require major reform. In the 1800s women actually had fewer rights than in colonial times. They had few political or legal rights. Women could not vote or hold public office. A woman's husband owned all of her property.

Women from New England to Ohio joined the antislavery societies. Many saw similarities between the treatment of enslaved persons and women.

Journalist Margaret Fuller observed that "there exists in the minds of men a tone of feeling toward women as towards slaves." Abolitionists Angelina and Sarah Grimké confronted this feeling when they spoke to antislavery groups. Audiences did not criticize their stand on slavery. They did, though, question their right to speak in public.

As a result, the Grimkés soon found themselves in the midst of "an entirely new contest—a contest for the rights of woman." Sarah wrote that "all I ask… is that [men] will take their feet from off our necks and permit us to stand upright."

QAR Characteristics

IN THE BOOK

Right There

Source:

The answer is found in the text.

The answer is easily found within a single statement or paragraph.

Wording:

The wording of the question is found in the text and may be repeated in the answer.

The answer may use the exact wording in the text.

Content:

The answer is usually a definition, a fact, or a detail from the text.

Format:

The question-answer format is usually multiple-choice.

Think and Search

Source:

The answer is found in the text.

The answer is found in more than one statement, paragraph, or section of the text.

Wording:

The wording of the question may or may not be found in the text.

The answer may or may not use the wording in the text.

Content:

The answer may require inferring or summarizing from information given in the text.

The answer may address the main idea of the text.

Format:

The question-answer format may be multiple-choice or short answer.

IN MY HEAD

Author and Me

Source:

The answer is based on my own knowledge and experience.

The answer combines an understanding of the text with my own knowledge or experience. It may connect to other texts I have read.

Wording:

The wording of the question is unlikely to be found in the text.

The answer may or may not use wording in the text. The answer may refer to or draw on points made in the text.

Content:

The answer is a narrative inferred from or based on information given in the text.

The answer addresses the main idea or theme of the text.

Format:

The question-answer format may be multiple-choice, short answer, or extended response (essay).

On My Own

Source:

The answer is based on my own knowledge and experience.

The answer is independent of the text. It is related to the general topic of the text but comes from my own experience, knowledge, and reading.

Wording:

The wording of the question is not found in the text.

The answer will not use wording in the text.

Content:

The answer is a personal narrative (explanation, opinion, description) related to the general topic or theme of the text.

Format:

The question-answer format is usually short answer or extended response (essay).

Concept Lesson 1   5

Directions: Reread the passage on page 3. Answer the questions and identify the QAR. On the next page, write the strategies you used to find the answers.

QUESTION / ANSWER / QAR

1. What did audiences of the antislavery speakers criticize?

   QAR: _____

2. What were some rights women lacked in the 1800s?

   QAR: _____

3. In this passage, the term *abolitionists* refers to what?

   QAR: _____

4. What is our society's attitude toward women's rights today?

   QAR: _____

Concept Lesson 1

STRATEGY

1.

2.

3.

4.

Concept Lesson 1

Directions: Write a short-answer question about the text on page 3 for each type of QAR. Then tell why the question represents that QAR.

Right There

Question	Answer	Why this is a Right There QAR

Think and Search

Question	Answer	Why this is a Think and Search QAR

Author and Me

Question	Answer	Why this is an Author and Me QAR

On My Own

Question	Answer	Why this is an On My Own QAR

Concept Lesson 1

Directions: Write four new questions about the text on page 3 in the spaces provided. (Do not fill in the answers.) When instructed to do so, exchange your *Student Activity Book* with a partner and answer each other's questions.

Partner's Name: _____

Directions: Answer each question, identify the QAR, and explain how you know what kind of QAR it is.

1.

Answer:

QAR:

How do you know:

2.

Answer:

QAR:

How do you know:

Concept Lesson 1

3.

   Answer:

   QAR:

   How do you know:

4.

   Answer:

   QAR:

   How do you know:

Directions: Read this passage from *Sue at the Field Museum*.

Sue the T-Rex

The first *T. rex* specimen was found in 1900. Since then, only seven skeletons that are more than half complete have been discovered. Of these, Sue is the largest, most complete, and best preserved *T. rex* ever found. Most of Sue's bones are in excellent condition and have a high degree of surface detail. Sixty-seven million years after her death, it is still possible to see fine details showing where muscles, tendons, and other soft tissues rested against or attached to the bone. Sue's completeness, combined with the exquisite preservation of the bones, makes her an invaluable scientific resource, permitting highly detailed study of *T. rex* anatomy.

In the summer of 1990, Sue Hendrickson was working as a fossil hunter with a commercial fossil-collecting team near Faith, South Dakota. On August 12 most of the team went into town to get a flat tire fixed and to take a short break from the heat. Sue stayed behind to look for fossils. She hiked over to some sandstone bluffs that had previously caught her attention. Within minutes she spotted some bone fragments on the ground. She scanned the cliffs above to find out where the fragments had fallen from and saw dinosaur bones—big ones. She climbed up the cliff for a better look at the bones, and saw they were huge. She thought she had found a *T. rex*, and when the team returned, they confirmed her find and promptly named it "Sue" in her honor.

Soon after Sue was discovered, her bones became the center of a dispute. Who owned the fossil?

To dig up dinosaurs, you always need the landowner's permission. But in Sue's case it was unclear whose land it was because . . . the bones were found on land that was part of a Sioux Indian reservation, BUT . . . the land belonged to a private rancher, BUT . . . the rancher was part Sioux, and his land was held in trust by the U.S. government. While people argued about who owned Sue, the bones were safely locked away in storerooms at the South Dakota School of Mines and Technology. In the end, a judge decided that Sue was held in trust by the U.S. government for the rancher on whose property the skeleton had been found. The rancher, in turn, decided to sell Sue at public auction.

Following the long custody battle, Sue was sold at Sotheby's auction house in New York on October 4, 1997. Just eight minutes after the bidding started, the Field Museum of Chicago purchased Sue for nearly $8.4 million—the most money ever paid for a fossil. On May 17, 2000, the Field Museum unveiled Sue, the largest, most complete, and best preserved *T. rex* fossil yet discovered.

Directions: Answer the questions below about the text on page 11. Then, identify the text structure and the strategy you used to find the answer.

QUESTION / ANSWER

1. Who found Sue?
   - **A.** A rancher
   - **B.** A hike
   - **C.** A professional fossil hunter
   - **D.** None of the above

2. What happened after Sue was found?
   - **A.** The ownership of the bones was contested.
   - **B.** The bones were temporarily stored at a university.
   - **C.** The bones were put on display at a museum.
   - **D.** All of the above.

3. Why was the ownership of the bones unclear?

4. Why was Sue an important find?

TEXT STRUCTURE	STRATEGY
1.	1.
2.	2.
3.	3.
4.	4.

Concept Lesson 2

Directions: Write two short-answer Think and Search questions about the text on page 11. Then for each question, write the answer, identify the text structure, and tell why the QAR is Think and Search.

1.

   Answer:

   Text Structure:

   Why this is a Think and Search QAR:

2.

   Answer:

   Text Structure:

   Why this is a Think and Search QAR:

Directions: Write two new questions about the text on page 11 in the spaces provided. (Do not fill in the answers.) When instructed to do so, exchange your *Student Activity Book* with a partner and answer each other's questions.

Partner's Name: _____

Directions: Answer each question, identify the QAR, explain how you know what kind of QAR it is, and identify the strategies you used.

1.

Answer:

QAR:

How do you know:

Strategies for finding the answer:

2.

Answer:

QAR:

How do you know:

Strategies for finding the answer:

Concept Lesson 2

In My Head Sample Questions

1. **Author and Me: Text to Self**
   - How would you feel if you were the main character?
   - Compare your experience with that of someone in the story.
   - How does the situation today reflect the outcome of events described in the text?

   Notes:

2. **Author and Me: Text to Text**
   - Compare the main character with a character in another text you have read. How is he or she the same or different?

   Notes:

3. **Author and Me: Text to Themes**
   - What is the theme of the story?
   - What do you think was the author's primary message to the reader?

   Notes:

4. **On My Own**
   - Do you think women have full civil rights? Why or why not? Explain your conclusion.
   - Describe a time when you were scared. Why were you frightened? What happened?

   Notes:

Directions: Read this excerpt from *The Red Badge of Courage: An Episode of the American Civil War* by Stephen Crane. Then answer the questions on the next page.

The Red Badge of Courage

The cold passed reluctantly from the earth, and the retiring fogs revealed an army stretched out on the hills, resting. As the landscape changed from brown to green, the army awakened, and began to tremble with eagerness at the noise of rumors….

Once a certain tall soldier developed virtues and went resolutely to wash a shirt. He came flying back from a brook waving his garment bannerlike. He was swelled with a tale he had heard from a reliable friend, who had heard it from a truthful cavalryman, who had heard it from his trustworthy brother, one of the orderlies at division headquarters. He adopted the important air of a herald in red and gold. "We're goin' t' move t' morrah—sure," he said pompously to a group in the company street. "We're goin' 'way up the river, cut across, an' come around in behint 'em."

To his attentive audience he drew a loud and elaborate plan of a very brilliant campaign. When he had finished, the blue-clothed men scattered into small arguing groups between the rows of squat brown huts…. "It's a lie! that's all it is—a thunderin' lie!" said another private loudly. His smooth face was flushed, and his hands were thrust sulkily into his trousers' pockets. He took the matter as an affront to him. "I don't believe the derned old army's ever going to move. We're set. I've got ready to move eight times in the last two weeks, and we ain't moved yet."

The tall soldier felt called upon to defend the truth of a rumor he himself had introduced. He and the loud one came near to fighting over it….

Many of the men engaged in a spirited debate. One outlined in a peculiarly lucid manner all the plans of the commanding general. He was opposed by men who advocated that there were other plans of campaign. They clamored at each other, numbers making futile bids for the popular attention. Meanwhile, the soldier who had fetched the rumor bustled about with much importance….

There was a youthful private who listened with eager ears to the words of the tall soldier and to the varied comments of his comrades. After receiving a fill of discussions concerning marches and attacks, he went to his hut and crawled through an intricate hole that served it as a door. He wished to be alone with some new thoughts that had lately come to him….

The youth was in a little trance of astonishment. So they were at last going to fight. On the morrow, perhaps, there would be a battle, and he would be in it. For a time he was obliged to labor to make himself believe. He could not accept with assurance an omen that he was about to mingle in one of those great affairs of the earth.

He had, of course, dreamed of battles all his life—of vague and bloody conflicts that had thrilled him with their sweep and fire. In visions he had seen himself in many struggles. He had imagined peoples secure in the shadow of his eagle-eyed prowess. But awake he had regarded battles as crimson blotches on the pages of the past. He had put them as things of the bygone with his thought-images of heavy crowns and high castles. There was a portion of the world's history which he had regarded as the time of wars, but it, he thought, had been long gone over the horizon and had disappeared forever.

Directions: Answer the following questions about the text on page 17. Indicate the type of QAR, where you found the answer, and the strategies you used to find the answer.

QUESTION / ANSWER / QAR

1. Describe how the soldiers responded to the rumor of battle and how you react to rumors or gossip that you hear.

   QAR: _____

2. The "youth" in this passage "was about to mingle in one of those great affairs of the earth." Compare this "great affair" with an event in another story you have read.

   QAR: _____

3. In this passage, one of the author's themes is

   A. how the uncertainty of war affected the soldiers
   B. people will believe anything they hear
   C. the soldiers were not afraid to die
   D. the virtues of bravery

   QAR: _____

4. What would it be like to be a soldier facing battle? What would your thoughts and concerns be?

   QAR: _____

Concept Lesson 3

SOURCE	STRATEGY
1.	1.
2.	2.
3.	3.
4.	4.

Directions: Write two short-answer In My Head questions about the text on page 17. Then write the answers and why the QAR categories are In My Head.

Question	Answer	Why this is an In My Head QAR

Question	Answer	Why this is an In My Head QAR

Directions: Write two new questions about the text on page 17 in the spaces provided. (Do not fill in the answers.) When instructed to do so, exchange your *Student Activity Book* with a partner and answer each other's questions.

Partner's Name: _____

Directions: Answer each question, identify the QAR, and explain how you know what type of QAR it is.

1.

   Answer:

   QAR:

   How do you know:

2.

   Answer:

   QAR:

   How do you know:

Concept Lesson 3

Test-Taking Strategies

Before you read the text…
- Read the test questions first.
- Scan for key words in the text.
- Skim first and last sentences; read the text quickly to find the main idea.

As you read…
- Circle, underline, or highlight key words or phrases.
- Identify important information and make notes.
- Predict what will happen next.
- Connect to the text. Ask yourself: What do I already know about this topic? What else have I read about this topic? Have I experienced something similar?
- Identify the theme.

Before you answer the question…
- Reread the question.
- Identify the QAR.
- Reread or skim the text.
- Scan your notes and words or phrases that you highlighted in the text.
- Brainstorm an answer and briefly note your thoughts. For an essay question, make a short outline of your answer.

For your answer…
- Summarize, infer, draw conclusions, or make connections.
- Support your answer with details from the text.
- Write complete sentences. Use conventional grammar, punctuation, and spelling.
- Pace yourself. Don't spend too much time on any one answer.

Directions: Read the following excerpt from *Ellen Foster* by Kaye Gibbons.

Chapter 1, Part 1

When I was little I would think of ways to kill my daddy…

He drank his own self to death the year after the County moved me out… And I can say for a fact that I am better off now than when he was alive.

I live in a clean brick house and mostly I am left to myself. When I start to carry an odor I take a bath and folks tell me how sweet I look.

There is a plenty to eat here and if we run out of something we just go to the store and get some more. I had me a egg sandwich for breakfast, mayonnaise on both sides. And I may fix me another one for lunch.

Two years ago I did not have much of anything. Not that I live in the lap of luxury now but I am proud for the schoolbus to pick me up here every morning. My stylish well-groomed self standing in the front yard with the grass green and the hedge bushes square.

I figure I made out pretty good considering the rest of my family is either dead or crazy…

Oh but I do remember when I was scared. Everything was so wrong like somebody had knocked something loose and my family was shaking itself to death. Some wild ride broke and the one in charge strolled off and let us spin and shake and fly off the rail. And they both died tired of the wild crazy spinning and wore out and sick…

Even my mama's skin looked tired of holding in her weak self. She would prop herself up by the refrigerator and watch my daddy go round the table swearing at all who did him wrong. She looked all sad in her face like it was all her fault.

She comes home from the hospital sometimes. If I was her I would stay there. All laid up in the air conditioning with folks patting your head and bringing you fruit baskets.

Oh no. She comes in and he lets into her right away. Carrying on. Set up in his E-Z lounger like he is King for a Day. You bring me this or that he might say.

She comes in the door and he asks about supper right off. What does she have planned? he wants to know. Wouldn't he like to know what I myself have planned?… More like a big mean baby than a grown man…

Big wind-up toy of a man. He is just too sorry to talk back to even if he is my daddy. And she is too limp and too sore to get up the breath to push the words out to stop it all. She just stands there and lets him work out his evil on her.

Get in the kitchen and fix me something to eat. I had to cook the whole time you was gone, he tells her.

And that was some lie he made up. Cook for his own self. Ha. If I did not feed us both we had to go into town and get take-out chicken. I myself was looking forward to something fit to eat but I was not about to say anything.

Directions: Complete this chart as you work together with your peers and teacher.

QUESTION / ANSWER / QAR

1. The relationship Ellen had with her dad was that
    A. he took care of her
    B. she took care of him
    C. she lived away from him
    D. she admired him

    QAR: _____

2. What has happened to Ellen in the past two years?

    QAR: _____

3. Compare Ellen's old life with her new life.

    QAR: _____

4. What does Ellen value most in life?

    QAR: _____

STRATEGY

1.

2.

3.

4.

Directions: Read more from *Ellen Foster*. Then answer the questions on pages 27 through 29.

Chapter 1, Part 2

Nobody yells after anybody to do this or that here.

My new mama lays out the food and we all take a turn to dish it out. Then we eat and have a good time. Toast or biscuits with anything you please. Eggs any style. Corn cut off the cob the same day we eat it. I keep my elbows off the table and wipe my mouth like a lady. …When everybody is done eating my new mama puts the dishes in a thing, shuts the door, cuts on it, and Wa-La they are clean

My mama does not say a word about being tired or sore. She did ask who kept everything so clean and he took the credit. I do not know who he thinks he fooled. I knew he lied and my mama did too. She just asked to be saying something.

Mama puts the food out on the table and he wants to know what I am staring at. At you humped over your plate like one of us is about to snatch it from you. You old hog. But I do not say it.

Why don't you eat? he wants to know.

I don't have an appetite, I say back.

Well, you better eat. Your mama looks like this might be her last supper.

He is so sure he's funny that he laughs at his own self…

Now at my new mama's I lay up late in the day and watch the rain fall outside. Not one thing is pressing on me to get done here.

I have a bag of candy to eat on. One piece at a time. Make it last. All I got left to do is eat supper and wash myself.

Look around my room. It is so nice.

When I accumulate enough money I plan to get some colored glass things that you dangle from the window glass. I lay here and feature how that would look. I already got pink checkerboard curtains with dingleballs around the edges. My new mama sewed them for me. She also sewed matching sacks that I cram my pillows into every morning.

Everything matches. It is all so neat and clean…

The yelling makes my mama jump and if she was asleep she is awake now. Grits her teeth every time he calls out damn this or that. The more he drinks the less sense he makes.

By the time the dog races come on he's stretched out on the bathroom floor and can't get up. I know I need to go in there and poke him. Same thing every Saturday…

I get up and go in there and tell him to get up that folks got to come in here and do their business.

He can go lay in the truck.

He just grunts and grabs at my ankle and misses.

Get on up I say again to him. You got to be firm when he is like this. He'd lay there and rot if I let him so I nudge him with my foot. I will not touch my hands to him. Makes me want to heave my own self seeing him pull himself up on the sink. He zig-zags out through the living room and

Chapter 1, Part 2 (continued)

I guess he makes it out the door. I don't hear him fall down the steps.

And where did she come from? Standing in the door looking at it all.

Get back in bed, I say to mama.

Mama's easy to tend to. She goes back in the bedroom. Not a bit of trouble. Just stiff and hard to move around. I get her back in the bed and tell her he's outside for the night. She starts to whimper and I say it is no reason to cry. But she will wear herself out crying.

I ought to lock him out.

A grown man that should be bringing her food to nibble on and books to look at. No but he is taking care of his own self tonight. Just like she is not sick or kin to him.

A storm is coming up. And I will lay here with my mama until I see her chest rise up and sink down regular. Deep and regular and far away from the man in the truck.

Directions: Answer the questions below and on the next two pages. Identify the QAR categories and the test-taking strategies you used.

1. Ellen is most upset that her father
   - **A.** doesn't work
   - **B.** abuses her mother
   - **C.** does not take care of her mother
   - **D.** does not take care of her

   QAR: _____

   Test-Taking Strategy:

2. Describe Ellen's feelings toward her father during the scene when her mother has returned home.

   QAR: _____
   Test-Taking Strategy:

Concept Lesson 4

3. What role has Ellen taken on in her birth family and why?

   QAR: _____
   Test-Taking Strategy:

4. Ellen's feelings toward her father could best be described as
   A. anger
   B. pity
   C. disgust
   D. A and B
   E. A and C
   QAR: _____
   Test-Taking Strategy:

5. Describe the stability and simple pleasures of Ellen's new life.

   QAR: _____
   Test-Taking Strategy:

6. If Ellen went to your school, what would you think of her? Give specific examples and reasons.

   QAR: _____
   Test-Taking Strategy:

7. Ellen's new life is like her old one because
   A. no one yells
   B. her mother takes care of her
   C. she has plenty to eat
   D. she lives in a messy place
   E. none of the above

   QAR: _____
   Test-Taking Strategy:

8. How does Ellen's birth mother react to her husband?

   QAR: _____
   Test-Taking Strategy:

9. Compare and contrast Ellen's new life with her old life. Use details from the story to support your answer.

   QAR: _____
   Test-Taking Strategy:

10. Ellen had to struggle to survive in her birth family. Describe a personal experience in which you struggled for success, happiness, stability, approval, or some other goal.

    QAR: _____
    Test-Taking Strategy:

Directions: Read the following article by Marcella J. Kehus.

The Complexities of Cloning

Before 1996, few people had actually considered cloning a real possibility beyond something you might read about or see in a science fiction movie. But in July of that year, when Dolly the ewe (baby sheep) was born as a clone of her mother, some great debates began that are still raging in many areas. Cloning, or the creating of a living replica from DNA from a body cell, took quite a long time to develop before it actually worked with Dolly as its first success. Now people from politicians to religious leaders to scientists and the general public continue to argue over whether this technology should be applied to humans. The basic debate comes down to: Should we or should we not allow the cloning of human beings? And, if we do so, what are the possible results?

Now that the procedure for cloning has been discovered, it seems only a matter of time before it is applied to humans. This is where a number of people, specialists and general citizens alike, have serious concerns. One of their primary concerns, which often comes up with every new technology, are the number of ways that such a technology might be abused. For example, what if a certain group wanted to use cloning to create an army of exact duplicate soldiers or creatures to carry out their evil deeds? And, because cloning can include genetic engineering, or selecting just the right genes to create a certain kind of being (strong, green eyes, etc.), the idea of creating a look-alike super-human race reminds people quickly of the terrible possibilities of Hitler-like beliefs if given the power of cloning.

There are lesser kinds of abuses that the power of human cloning could inspire. Perhaps a former football player got his career cut short due to an injury; what would keep him from creating a clone of himself to play and become the star he always wanted to be? Cloning could become a fashionable way for other conceited people to just re-create themselves and the result may be a child who is never given a chance to become an individual.

On the other hand, there are impressive possibilities when it comes to human cloning. First, cloning is another possible solution for couples who are otherwise unable to have children of their own. In fact, the medical solutions made possible by clones are numerous including the supplying of life-saving transplant organs or bone marrow by cloned family members that would automatically match. And, when coupled with genetic engineering, cloning may allow us to create better humans as we discover more and more about disease and aging and produce clones who are better-equipped to survive.

Certainly, the possibilities of human cloning are scientifically possible. Yet, as with other new developments, one must carefully consider the possible outcomes—both good and bad. Ultimately, we as a society will make the decision as to whether human cloning's benefits outweigh its possible abuses and where we go from here.

Directions: Answer the following questions about the article on page 30 and identify each QAR.

1. According to the article, what "great debate" started in 1996?

   QAR: _____

2. What are other arguments against cloning that are not mentioned in the article?

   QAR: _____

3. Who is involved in the debate about human cloning?

   QAR: _____

4. What do you think is the strongest reason given for human cloning? Why?

   QAR: _____

Concept Lesson 5

5. What do you think is the strongest reason against human cloning? Why?

   QAR: _____

6. What are three different ways that individuals might benefit from human cloning?

   QAR: _____

7. Who do you think will make the final decision about whether or not human cloning is allowed?

   QAR: _____

Essay-Writing Tips, Part 1

- Before you start writing, identify the QAR.

- Create a short outline of your main thesis or idea and two or three main points that support your thesis. If you're stuck, do some brainstorming.

- Restate the question as a thesis or opening line(s).

- Answer all parts of the question. Check off each part as you go.

- For each part of the answer, note the specific part in the text that supports it.

- Include an introduction, at least two body paragraphs, and a conclusion.

- Present your ideas in a logical way. What comes first, second, third? What is your conclusion?

- If you have time, reread your essay to correct spelling, punctuation, or grammatical errors.

Directions: Reread the passage on page 30. Then choose a side for or against human cloning and write an essay to convince your audience to believe as you do.

Directions: Read "The Bungee Lunge" on pages 36 and 37. As you read, write five during reading questions in the spaces below. Identify the QAR that each question represents.

1.

   QAR: _____

2.

   QAR: _____

3.

   QAR: _____

4.

   QAR: _____

5.

   QAR: _____

Booster Lesson 1

Directions: Read this article by Karen McNulty.

The Bungee Lunge

Here's your giant rubber band. Now jump! It's only a 10-story plunge—and science will spring you back.

The Science Behind the Bounce

Ready?

When standing high on a jump platform, you have lots of potential (stored) energy.

Jump!

Leap off and your potential energy is converted to kinetic energy, the energy of motion. For a few seconds, you experience free fall, until there's no more slack in the cord.

Stret – t – ch

Then the cord starts to stretch. This stores the energy of your fall in the cord.

Bounce

This stored energy springs you back up. You fall and bounce again… and again…

Phew!

Each bounce disperses some of your energy, so eventually you stop. You'll have to hang around until someone lowers you to a raft or the ground.

You're hanging onto the railing of a bridge, 46 m above the river. Your friends on the bank below seem awfully small; looking at them makes you dizzy. Someone standing behind you is counting down "Three…two…one!" Defying every sane notion in your brain, you leap—headfirst.

The 100 km/h fall toward the water terrifies you. But just as you close your eyes for the icy plunge, something happens: You bounce back!

Better thank your lucky *bungee cord*—that wrist-thick band of latex rubber strapped to your ankles and anchored to the bridge. Because it was the right length, it kept you high and dry. And because it stret-t-t-ched and recoiled—giving you a few good bounces—it used up the energy of your fall so you didn't get torn limb from limb. Phew!

Those who have done it say it's the thrill of a lifetime—"a natural high." Others call it crazy. But everyone knows it as "bungee jumping," the sport springing up (and down) across the nation.

At least one group of people has been "bungee jumping" for ages: the men of Pentecost Island in the South Pacific. They make cords from elastic vines, lash them to their ankles, and plunge off wooden towers into pits of softened earth. For these islanders, jumping is a springtime ritual, meant to demonstrate courage and supposedly ensure a plentiful yam harvest.

In North America, jumpers take the bungee plunge just for the excitement of it. Scott Bergman, who runs a bungee-jumping company in California, explains the appeal. "It's a feeling of having absolutely no control—and loving it."

And it doesn't take any skill. Just $75 to $100 and *faith*—in physics. It's a simple physics equation, after all, that let's "jump masters" like Bergman determine how far the cord will stretch when you take the plunge—whether it will stretch too far.

The Bungee Lunge (continued)

Weighing the Odds

The major variables are the stretchiness, or *elasticity*, of the cord—predetermined by the manufacturer—and the jumper's weight. As you might guess, "the heavier you are, the more the cord is going to stretch," says physicist Peter Brancazio.

By weighing customers (they don't just ask), using the equation, and adjusting cords, jump masters have bounced thousands to safety. (There have been some deaths—usually caused by frayed cords or other faulty equipment.)

Jump experts can even adjust the cords to give their clients custom-made thrills. "When we jump off bridges in California," says Bergman, "we ask the people if they want to just touch the water, dunk their heads in, or go all the way. We can really get it that exact."

Really? "I wouldn't trust them," says Brancazio, "but I guess they can."

If, for example, Bergman calculates that you'll crack your skull on a rock in the river, he can shorten your cord. "That starts the stretch at a higher point off the ground," says Brancazio.

Or you can jump with two cords. "In that case," says Brancazio, your weight is "equally divided between the cords so each stretches half as far."

Chances are, you'll scream just as hard with fear and delight.

Directions: Write a short answer to the following questions based on the article on pages 36 and 37 and identify the QAR for each.

1. Explain how energy is stored and released in a bungee cord.

   QAR: _____

2. Summarize the points of view of the two experts (Scott Bergman and Peter Brancazio) quoted in the article. Why might they have different perspectives on bungee jumping?

   QAR: _____

3. Would you ever consider bungee jumping? What would be your major considerations in making a decision?

   QAR: _____

4. Compare bungee jumping in the South Pacific to California.

   QAR: _____

5. Compare the during reading questions you wrote on page 35 with the questions above. What types of QAR categories are there? Which of your questions prepared you for the questions asked above, if any?

   QAR: _____

38 Booster Lesson 1

Tips for Using Textbooks

Look at text features:

- Headings and subheadings
- Summaries (main idea, key points)
- Terms and their definitions
- Words bolded or highlighted in the text
- Captions for illustrations

Use previewing techniques:

- Preview comprehension questions or exercises at the end.
- Skim the first and last sentences of each paragraph.

Take notes and ask questions:

- Restate definitions and explanations in your own words.
- Connect to the text: What do I already know? What do I want to learn?
- Restate or paraphrase questions in your own words.

Directions: Read this passage from *American History: The Early Years to 1877*.

The Women's Rights Movement

Guide to Reading

Main Idea
Emboldened by their work in the antislavery movement, many women fought to improve their own status in society.

Read to Learn...
* why women became unhappy with their positions in the mid-1800s
* how working in the antislavery movement prepared women to fight for their own rights
* what arguments opponents used against the women's rights movement

Terms to Know
* abolitionist
* suffrage

Women took a special interest in the antislavery movement. As they fought for social reform for African Americans, they realized that they also lacked full social and political rights. When women such as Angelina and Sarah Grimké tried to participate actively in the antislavery movement, they often met resistance. As a result, many abolitionists became crusaders for women's rights.

Equal rights for women would require major reform. In the 1800s women actually had fewer rights than in colonial times. They had few political or legal rights. Women could not vote. They could not hold public office. A woman's husband owned all her property.

Antislavery Movement Gives Women a Boost

Women from New England to Ohio joined the antislavery societies. They worked hard, gathering signatures on thousands of petitions to send to Congress. They also read about and discussed the abuses of slavery. Many saw similarities between the treatment of enslaved persons and women.

In her book *Woman in the Nineteenth Century*, journalist **Margaret Fuller** observed that "there exists in the minds of men a tone of feeling toward women as towards slaves." Abolitionists Angelina and Sarah Grimké confronted this feeling when they spoke to antislavery groups. Audiences did not criticize their stand on slavery. They did, though, question their right to speak in public.

As a result, the Grimkés soon found themselves in the midst of "an entirely new contest—a contest for the rights of woman." Sarah wrote that "all I ask... is that [men] will take their feet from off our necks and permit us to stand upright."

The Women's Rights Movement

Their involvement in the antislavery movement and other reform movements gave women roles outside their homes and families. They learned valuable skills, such as organizing, working

Booster Lesson 2

The Women's Rights Movement (continued)

together, and speaking in public. Eventually they used these skills to further their own cause—the women's rights movement.

In 1840 nine women from the United States attended the World Anti-Slavery Convention in **London**. When the women arrived at the convention, however, the male delegates barred them from participating. The women and some male allies protested. On the first day of the convention, delegates debated the situation.

Clergy at the convention considered it improper for women to participate. Other male delegates declared women "unfit for public or business meetings." In the end, the majority of delegates decided that women could not take part in discussions. Instead, the women delegates would have to sit in the gallery behind a curtain.

Humiliated and angry, two of the women, Lucretia Coffin Mott and Elizabeth Cady Stanton, spent hours after the meetings talking about women's position in society. They realized that they could not bring about social change if they themselves lacked social and political rights. Stanton and Mott "resolved to hold a convention as soon as we returned home, and form a society to advocate the rights of women."

The Seneca Falls Convention

Eight years passed before the two friends organized their convention. On July 19, 1848, the first women's rights convention opened in Seneca Falls, New York. Both male and female delegates attended the convention. The delegates issued the Seneca Falls Declaration, which proclaimed that "all men and women are created equal."

Then the declaration listed several resolutions. One of them demanded suffrage, or the right to vote, for women. Even supporters of women's rights hesitated to pass this bold demand. Mott exclaimed, "Oh, Lizzie, thou will make us ridiculous! We must go slowly." But Stanton refused to withdraw the resolution. After much heated debate, it passed by a narrow margin.

The Seneca Falls Convention marked the beginning of an organized women's rights movement. Following the convention, women did not achieve all of their demands. They did, however, overcome some obstacles. Many states passed laws permitting women to own their own property and keep their earnings. Many men and women, though, continued to oppose the movement. Most politicians ignored or acted hostile to the issue of women's rights.

The Women's Rights Movement (continued)

Assessment

Check for Understanding
1. Define suffrage.
2. Why did women become unhappy with their position in the mid-1800s? About what areas of their daily lives were they most concerned?

Critical Thinking
3. **Comparing and Contrasting.** Contrast the views of the men and women who opposed the women's rights movement with those who supported it.

4. **Identifying Relationships.** Re-create the diagram shown here, and list how women's work in the antislavery movement prepared them to fight for their own rights.

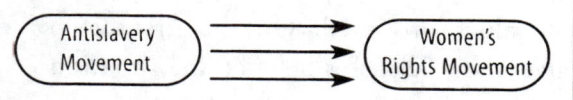

Antislavery Movement → Women's Rights Movement

Interdisciplinary Activity
5. **Citizenship.** Are women today denied any rights that men have? Draw up an agenda for a new Seneca Falls Convention listing topics for discussion.

Directions: Read "The Women's Rights Movement" on pages 40 and 41 and answer the questions from the Assessment section on page 42. Identify the type of QAR each question represents.

1.

   QAR: _____

2.

   QAR: _____

3.

   QAR: _____

4.

   QAR: _____

5.

   Write your agenda on a separate sheet or in your "QAR Reflections Journal."

   QAR: _____

Booster Lesson 2

Directions: Read this letter to President Franklin D. Roosevelt.

Dear Mr. President

Phila., Pa.
November 26, 1934

Honorable Franklin D. Roosevelt
Washington, D.C.

Dear Mr. President:

I am forced to write to you because we find ourselves in a very serious condition. For the last three or four years we have had depression and suffered with my family and little children severely. Now Since the Home Owners Loan Corporation opened up, I have been going up there in order to save my home, because there has been unemployment in my house for more than three years. You can imagine that I and my family have suffered from lack of water supply in my house for more than two years. Last winter I did not have coal and the pipes burst in my house and therefore could not make heat in the house. Now winter is here again and we are suffering of cold, no water in the house, and we are facing to be forced out of the house, because I have no money to move or pay so much money as they want when after making settlement. I am mother of little children, am sick and losing my health, and we are eight people in the family, and where can I go when I don't have money because no one is working in my house. The Home Loan Corporation wants $42. a month rent or else we will have to be on the street. I am living in this house for about ten years and when times were good we would put our last cent in the house and now I have no money, no home and no wheres to go. I beg of you to please help me and my family and little children for the sake of a sick mother and a suffering family to give this your immediate attention so we will not be forced to move or put out in the street.

Waiting and Hoping that you will act quickly.
Thanking you very much I remain

Mrs. E. L.

Directions: Read this excerpt from a speech by Robert Kennedy.

On the Death of Dr. Martin Luther King

This speech was given by Robert F. Kennedy on April 4, 1968, shortly after Dr. Martin Luther King, Jr. had been assassinated. At the time, Robert Kennedy was a U.S. Senator leading a race for the presidency, but he was assassinated a few months later.

Martin Luther King dedicated his life to love and to justice between fellow human beings. He died in the cause of that effort. In this difficult day, in this difficult time for the United States, it's perhaps well to ask what kind of a nation we are and what direction we want to move in.

For those of you who are black—considering the evidence evidently is that there were white people who were responsible—you can be filled with bitterness, and with hatred, and a desire for revenge.

We can move in that direction as a country, in greater polarization—black people amongst blacks, and white amongst whites, filled with hatred toward one another. Or we can make an effort, as Martin Luther King did, to understand and to comprehend, and replace that violence, that stain of bloodshed that has spread across our land, with an effort to understand, compassion and love.

For those of you who are black and are tempted to be filled with hatred and mistrust of the injustice of such an act, against all white people, I would only say that I can also feel in my own heart the same kind of feeling. I had a member of my family killed, but he was killed by a white man.

But we have to make an effort in the United States, we have to make an effort to understand, to get beyond these rather difficult times.

My favorite poet was Aeschylus. He once wrote: "Even in our sleep, pain which cannot forget falls drop by drop upon the heart, until, in our own despair, against our will, comes wisdom through the awful grace of God."

What we need in the United States is not division; what we need in the United States is not hatred; what we need in the United States is not violence and lawlessness, but is love and wisdom, and compassion toward one another, and a feeling of justice toward those who still suffer within our country, whether they be white or whether they be black.

So I ask you tonight to return home, to say a prayer for the family of Martin Luther King, yeah that's true, but more importantly to say a prayer for our own country, which all of us love—a prayer for understanding and that compassion of which I spoke. We can do well in this country. We will have difficult times. We've had difficult times in the past. And we will have difficult times in the future. It is not the end of violence; it is not the end of lawlessness; and it's not the end of disorder.

But the vast majority of white people and the vast majority of black people in this country want to live together, want to improve the quality of our life, and want justice for all human beings that abide in our land.

Let us dedicate ourselves to what the Greeks wrote so many years ago: to tame the savageness of man and make gentle the life of this world.

Let us dedicate ourselves to that, and say a prayer for our country and for our people.

Directions: Read pages 44 and 45 and then answer the following questions. Identify the QAR after your answer.

1. Compare and contrast the audience, purpose, and writing style of the two passages.

   QAR: _____

2. If you were President Roosevelt, how would you have responded to Mrs. E. L.'s letter? Why?

   QAR: _____

3. What would have been your reaction to Robert F. Kennedy's speech at the time. Why?

   QAR: _____

Best-Answer Strategies

IN THE BOOK

Right There
- Reread.
- Scan for key words.
- Recall key facts or figures.

Think and Search
- Reread.
- Scan for key words.
- Skim first and last sentences.
- Identify important information.
- Look for specific examples.
- Identify characters or people, events, plot, problem and solutions, etc.
- Identify the main idea or theme.
- Predict what will happen next.

IN MY HEAD

Author and Me
- Reread.
- Skim first and last sentences.
- Connect to important information What do I already know about this subject?
- Connect to the characters or people and events in the text.
- Connect to the main idea or theme.
- Predict what will happen next.
- Connect to other texts. What have I read before on this same subject or with this same theme?

On My Own
- Reread.
- Connect to the general theme or topic.
- Connect to other texts. What have I read before on this same subject or with this same theme?

Directions: Read this passage from *Lasers* by Lynne Kelly and answer the questions on page 49.

How a Laser Beam Is Made

The first pulse laser was made by Theodore H. Maiman of the United States in 1960. He used a ruby rod to make a short flash of laser light. The method has been improved since then, but the idea is the same.

1. A rod of ruby, about the size of a finger is used. Real ruby is very expensive, but synthetic ruby can be used.

2. The ends of the ruby rod are ground so they are perfectly smooth and parallel to each other. Each end is painted silver to make mirrors, but one end receives a thinner layer of paint than the other. This means that this end is only partially reflective.

3. A flash tube is wrapped around the ruby rob and connected to a battery. The flash tube and battery act as the power source.

4. When the flash tube is switched on, it produces bright, white light. This excites, or increases, the energy level of chromium atoms in the ruby. Light is reflected back and forth along the rod.

5. After a fraction of a second, a bright flash of red laser light will come out of the end of the ruby rod.

When the flash tube is switched on, chromium atoms in the ruby rod absorb some of the light energy. These atoms then give out energy again in the form of colored light. Light beams given out from one sort of atom that has been excited in this way will all be identical.

These identical light beams reflect back and forth along the ruby rod from one mirror to the other. As they do so, they excite more atoms, which give off more light. This goes on until the light beam has grown strong enough to break through the thinner mirror. All the light beams emitted from the thinner mirror will be identical and coherent and will travel in a straight line. They will be a laser beam.

The name *laser* comes from the way in which a laser beam is made. It is a form of light that is the result of many reflections between the mirrors on the ends of the ruby rod. This causes the energy to increase, or amplify. The chromium atoms that give off the pure light beam have been excited, or stimulated, by the flash of light. The atoms give out, or emit, pure monochromatic light, which is a form of electromagnetic radiation.

So a laser beam is the result of **Light Amplification** by **Stimulated Emission** of **Radiation**.

Directions: Answer the following questions about the text on page 48.

1. Which list includes the items used in generating laser light?
    A. ruby rod, flash tube, light switch
    B. synthetic ruby, mirrors, chromium atoms
    C. ruby rod, flash tube, battery
    D. ruby rod, reflective coating, flash tube, battery

2. What is the purpose of the mirrors at each end of the rod?
    A. They intensify the energy of the light beams as the light beams reflect back and forth between the mirrors.
    B. The protect the ends of the ruby rod as the high energy light beams travel back and forth.
    C. They decrease the level of energy of the chromium atoms in the ruby.
    D. None of the above.

3. What is the purpose of the flash tube and battery?
    A. They hold the ruby rod in place.
    B. They excite the chromium atoms.
    C. They make the light beams coherent.
    D. They generate the power needed to produce the energy for the laser beam.

4. How is a laser beam made?

5. Choose question 1, 2, or 3 above and analyze each response (A, B, C, D). Is it correct, partially correct, or incorrect? Why? Identify a statement or section of the passage that supports your answer.

Booster Lesson 4

The Road Not Taken

Two roads diverged in a yellow wood,
And sorry I could not travel both
And be one traveler, long I stood
And looked down one as far as I could
To where it bent in the undergrowth;

Then took the other, as just as fair,
And having perhaps the better claim,
Because it was grassy and wanted wear;
Though as for that the passing there
Had worn them really about the same,

And both that morning equally lay
In leaves no step had trodden black.
Oh, I kept the first for another day!
Yet knowing how way leads on to way,
I doubted if I should ever come back.

I shall be telling this with a sigh
Somewhere ages and ages hence:
Two roads diverged in a wood, and I—
I took the one less traveled by,
And that has made all the difference.

by Robert Frost

Life

They told me that Life could be just what I made it—
    Life could be fashioned and worn like a gown;
I, the designer; mine the decision
    Whether to wear it with bonnet or crown.

And so I selected the prettiest pattern—
    Life should be made of the rosiest hue—
Something unique, and a bit out of fashion,
    One that perhaps would be chosen by few.

But other folks came and they leaned o'er my shoulder;
    Somebody questioned the ultimate cost;
Somebody tangled the thread I was using;
    One day I found that my scissors were lost.

And somebody claimed the material faded;
    Somebody said I'd be tired ere 'twas worn;
Somebody's fingers, too pointed and spiteful,
    Snatched at the cloth, and I saw it was torn.

Oh! somebody tried to do all the sewing,
    Wanting always to advise or condone.
Here is my life, the product of many;
    Where is that gown I could fashion—alone?

by Nan Terrell Reed

Directions: This test has two parts. When you're finished with Part 1, go on to Part 2.

Part 1

Directions: Read the poems on page 50 and 51. Then write five Author and Me questions (connecting self to text, text to text, and text to theme) about the poems.

Author and Me Questions
for "The Road Not Taken"

1.

2.

3.

4.

5.

Author and Me Questions
for "Life"

1.

2.

3.

4.

5.

Booster Lesson 5

Part 2

Directions: Answer the following questions about the two poems. Support your answers with details from the text. Identify the QAR after each answer.

1. In "The Road Not Taken," how did the narrator know that one of the roads was "less traveled by"?

   QAR: _____

2. Why did the narrator choose "the road less traveled by"?

   QAR: _____

3. How does the narrator feel about his decision?

   QAR: _____

Booster Lesson 5

Part 2, continued

4. What is the main idea or theme of "The Road Not Taken"?

   QAR: _____

5. In the poem "Life," what does the author compare life to? What did she want her life to be like?

   QAR: _____

6. Who is the "Somebody" referred to in the poem? What does this somebody do?

   QAR: _____

7. At the end of "Life," how does the narrator feel about her life?

   QAR: _____

Part 2, continued

8. What is the main idea or theme of "Life"?

   QAR: _____

9. Compare and contrast the narrators of the poems "The Road Not Taken" and "Life." What were they seeking? How did they feel about their "road taken" and "gown" at the end?

   QAR: _____

10. Compare and contrast the main ideas or themes in each poem. How are they different? How are they similar?

    QAR: _____

Solving Math Story Problems

Ask yourself...

1. **What is given?**

   Identify the information already stated or given in the problem.

2. **What am I supposed to figure out?**

   Restate the problem in terms of the unknown quantity.

3. **What is the math concept?**

   Identify the math concept or concepts you have to know. What have you already learned about this concept?

Do the work...

4. **Set up the problem.**

   > Always show your work. If you get an incorrect answer because of a computation error, you may get partial credit for setting up the problem correctly and showing how you got the answer.

5. **Do the calculation.**

6. **Select or write your answer.**

Directions: Answer the following question. Refer to the steps on page 56 if necessary.

In Malia's eighth-grade class, 3 out of 5 students are girls. In a class of 30 students, how many are girls?

A. 12
B. 18
C. 20
D. 22

1. What is given?

2. What am I supposed to figure out?

3. What is the math concept?

4. Set up the problem.

5. Do the calculation.

6. Select or write your answer.

Booster Lesson 6

Essay-Writing Tips, Part 2

Purpose

Identify the purpose of the essay:
- Narration
- Information
- Persuasion

Audience

Identify who you are writing for.

Text Type

Identify the text type:
- Formal essay
- Letter
- Editorial
- Newspaper or journal article
- Procedure
- Others

Evaluation

- **Development:** Are the ideas well developed? Does the essay have good supporting or descriptive details?
- **Organization:** Is the essay well organized? Does it have good transitions between ideas and paragraphs?
- **Use of language:** Is the sentence structure varied? Is descriptive or figurative language used effectively?
- **Mechanics:** Do grammatical, spelling, and punctuation errors interfere with understanding the content?

Directions: Complete this worksheet as you work together with your peers and teacher.

ESSAY-WRITING WORKSHEET

Write an article for the school newspaper explaining the benefits of playing computer games.

QAR:

Purpose:

Audience:

Text Type:

Brainstorm Ideas:

Outline:

Booster Lesson 7

Directions: With a partner, complete the worksheet. Then write your letter on the next page.

ESSAY-WRITING WORKSHEET

Think of a social issue affecting your school, neighborhood, or community (for example, pollution, noise, litter, homelessness, traffic, etc.). Write a letter to a public official describing the problem and asking for help. Explain what you think should be done to solve it and why.

QAR:

Purpose:

Audience:

Text Type:

Brainstorm Ideas:

Outline:

Directions: Use this page to write your letter.

Directions: Complete this worksheet and write your essay on the next page.

ESSAY-WRITING WORKSHEET

Imagine that you just saw on the news that computer scientists have perfected the technologies behind artificial intelligence and expect manufacturers to begin making robots soon with many—but not all—human capabilities.

Explain what you and your family members would like robots to do if you could buy them. What kinds of things do you think the robots should or should not do?

QAR:

Purpose:

Audience:

Text Type:

Brainstorm Ideas:

Outline:

Directions: Use this page to write your essay.

Booster Lesson 7

Directions: Read the following article from *Teen Vogue*, as told to Sarah Brown by Bess Judson. Then answer the questions on pages 66 through 69.

Survivor

I noticed the bump during the summer. I thought it was cool the way it moved when I swallowed, like a seed sliding under the skin of an orange slice. I made my mom touch it. "Maybe it's a tumor!" I said, laughing. "It's probably just a swollen gland or something. We'll get it checked out if it doesn't go away soon," she said, and sent me off to school.

I was psyched to go to college... My first semester at Hamilton, in upstate New York, was so much fun. I joined the rugby team and started feeling really good about myself again.

I didn't even think about my bump until Christmas break, when I switched from a pediatrician to a general practitioner, who gave me a complete physical. As soon as she felt the lump on my thyroid she sent me for a needle biopsy. I thought it was routine, although I was surprised I went for tests right away, instead of having to schedule an appointment.

And then I went back to school. The first night I was back, my doctor called. The tumor was malignant. I had cancer, and in one week, I was scheduled to have an operation to remove my thyroid. I hung up the phone thinking back to the pink fluid the doctor had removed from my bump during the biopsy. The liquid had looked so harmless inside the syringe, like water used to clean a red paintbrush.

I was totally petrified. As soon as you hear that word—*cancer*—no one knows what to say. Doctors don't really even know that much about it. All they can do is try to cut it out.

My surgeon told me I'd need to take two weeks off from school, which is what I'd planned to do. I spent two nights in the hospital, in and out of sleep. Every few hours a man who called himself the Vampire would wake me up to draw my blood. When I finally stood up to walk, I had to hold my mother's arm to stay on my feet. I inched through the halls, rolling my IV beside me like a fish dragging the rod that hooked it....

Your thyroid is a gland in your neck—the part of your body that regulates metabolism (the physical and chemical processes that essentially maintain life). It also controls a lot of your hormones, and for about a month, I was just miserable. After surgery, I had to wait awhile before I could start taking thyroid-replacement hormones (which simulate the way an actual thyroid works), so my entire hormonal makeup was out of whack. I was tired and I was sad and I would cry all the time about nothing. I was what they call hypothyroid—I felt sluggish and just really crummy.

When I was finally allowed to start taking Synthroid (synthetic thyroid hormones), I was expecting to feel normal right away—to go back to classes and to play rugby in the spring. They have to raise the hormones to the right levels incrementally, so in the beginning, I was taking only about half the level I am now. I went back to school, and I did play rugby, but let's just say I wasn't a huge success. I was so much slower than I'd been before. My friends were totally supportive—they couldn't believe I was playing at all. I signed up for a full course load, but I ended up having to drop a class. In the fall semester, I'd gotten some C's and a D... but this time, somehow, I got straight A's. I think I was just happy to be back, happy I was able to pull through and rebound...

Survivor (continued)

I spent the spring and summer of my junior year studying in Spain. Seeing a different side of life—a side I'd never been exposed to before—gave me a new sense of perspective and taught me not to take so much for granted. When I got back, I knew I wanted to keep learning Spanish—to become fluent to the level of a native speaker, and to do something to help people along the way, if I could.... I had always thought about joining the Peace Corps, but I was never sure I could actually do it...

By my senior year, the more I thought about all the things I'd done, the more I knew that this time, I was strong enough to handle an experience like the Peace Corps. The hardest parts of my life have made me feel the most whole and the proudest of myself. I guess I needed to beat cancer to find out that I can do anything.

Directions: Answer the following questions about the article "Survivor."

1. The subject of "Survivor" was diagnosed with
   A. cancer of the blood (leukemia)
   B. cancer of the thyroid
   C. cancer of the throat
   D. hyperthyroidism
   E. none of the above

2. The thyroid works to regulate your metabolism or
   A. speed of body processes
   B. growth over a lifetime
   C. organ functions
   D. fighting off of disease
   E. none of the above

3. A *biopsy* is
   A. a gland in your neck
   B. a complete physical exam
   C. a procedure to extract blood or tissue from the body for analysis
   D. a drug that regulates your hormones
   E. a needle

4. Some of the symptoms of hypothyroidism are
   A. low energy
   B. depression or sadness
   C. sleeplessness
   D. A and B
   E. A and C

5. Thyroid replacement hormones
    A. cause hormonal imbalance
    B. are called Synthroid
    C. make you feel tired
    D. are effective right away
    E. simulate the way the thyroid works

6. Describe the events in Bess's life leading up to her decision to go into the Peace Corps.

7. Describe how Bess's battle with cancer affected her physically and emotionally. How was her academic and social life affected?

8. How did Bess feel about her experience with cancer?

Booster Lesson 8

9. Write an essay describing an experience in which you, someone you know, or a person or character you have read about was a "survivor." What was the experience? How did you or that person or character handle the experience? What were its impacts? What did the experience teach you (or the person or character)?

10. The Peace Corps is a government agency that sends volunteers to developing countries to assist communities in setting up businesses, to teach English, to train health care workers, to plant trees, and to do many other activities depending on the needs of the host country.

Write a letter of application to join the Peace Corps as if you were Bess Judson of "Survivor." Describe why you are a good candidate and the reasons they should accept your application.

QAR Reflections Journal

_____
_____
_____
_____
_____

QAR Reflections Journal

QAR Reflections Journal

QAR Reflections Journal

SUPER™ QAR

for Test-Wise Students

Student Activity Book

This book belongs to:

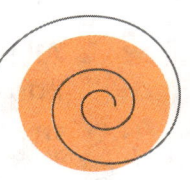

Wright Group

The McGraw·Hill Companies

Question Answer Relationships

In the Book

Right There

The answer is "right there" in the text. It is often a detail question.

Think and Search

The answer is in the text and involves cross-text searches. Identifying text structures such as the following helps organize your answer.

- Simple List
- Explanation
- Sequence
- Compare and Contrast
- Cause and Effect
- Problem and Solution

In My Head

Author and Me

The information to answer the question comes from background knowledge. You need to read the text and understand the question and you need to make connections.

- **Text to Self:** How the text affects the way you think or believe.
- **Text to Text:** Make connections with different texts you've read.
- **Text to Themes:** Use what you've read to generalize, identify themes, or interpret text.

On My Own

All the ideas and information to answer the question come from background knowledge, experiences, and beliefs. The question can be answered without reading the text.

Directions: Read this passage from *American History: The Early Years to 1877* by Donald A. Ritchie and Albert S. Broussard.

The Women's Rights Movement

Women took a special interest in the antislavery movement. As they fought for social reform for African Americans, they realized that they also lacked full social and political rights. When women tried to participate in the antislavery movement, they often met resistance. As a result, many abolitionists became crusaders for women's rights.

Equal rights for women would require major reform. In the 1800s women actually had fewer rights than in colonial times. They had few political or legal rights. Women could not vote or hold public office. A woman's husband owned all of her property.

Women from New England to Ohio joined the antislavery societies. Many saw similarities between the treatment of enslaved persons and women.

Journalist Margaret Fuller observed that "there exists in the minds of men a tone of feeling toward women as towards slaves." Abolitionists Angelina and Sarah Grimké confronted this feeling when they spoke to antislavery groups. Audiences did not criticize their stand on slavery. They did, though, question their right to speak in public.

As a result, the Grimkés soon found themselves in the midst of "an entirely new contest—a contest for the rights of woman." Sarah wrote that "all I ask… is that [men] will take their feet from off our necks and permit us to stand upright."

Concept Lesson 1

QAR Characteristics

IN THE BOOK

Right There

Source:

The answer is found in the text.

The answer is easily found within a single statement or paragraph.

Wording:

The wording of the question is found in the text and may be repeated in the answer.

The answer may use the exact wording in the text.

Content:

The answer is usually a definition, a fact, or a detail from the text.

Format:

The question-answer format is usually multiple-choice.

Think and Search

Source:

The answer is found in the text.

The answer is found in more than one statement, paragraph, or section of the text.

Wording:

The wording of the question may or may not be found in the text.

The answer may or may not use the wording in the text.

Content:

The answer may require inferring or summarizing from information given in the text.

The answer may address the main idea of the text.

Format:

The question-answer format may be multiple-choice or short answer.

IN MY HEAD

Author and Me

Source:

The answer is based on my own knowledge and experience.

The answer combines an understanding of the text with my own knowledge or experience. It may connect to other texts I have read.

Wording:

The wording of the question is unlikely to be found in the text.

The answer may or may not use wording in the text. The answer may refer to or draw on points made in the text.

Content:

The answer is a narrative inferred from or based on information given in the text.

The answer addresses the main idea or theme of the text.

Format:

The question-answer format may be multiple-choice, short answer, or extended response (essay).

On My Own

Source:

The answer is based on my own knowledge and experience.

The answer is independent of the text. It is related to the general topic of the text but comes from my own experience, knowledge, and reading.

Wording:

The wording of the question is not found in the text.

The answer will not use wording in the text.

Content:

The answer is a personal narrative (explanation, opinion, description) related to the general topic or theme of the text.

Format:

The question-answer format is usually short answer or extended response (essay).

Concept Lesson 1

Directions: Reread the passage on page 3. Answer the questions and identify the QAR. On the next page, write the strategies you used to find the answers.

QUESTION / ANSWER / QAR

1. What did audiences of the antislavery speakers criticize?

   QAR: _____

2. What were some rights women lacked in the 1800s?

   QAR: _____

3. In this passage, the term *abolitionists* refers to what?

   QAR: _____

4. What is our society's attitude toward women's rights today?

   QAR: _____

Concept Lesson 1

STRATEGY

1.

2.

3.

4.

Directions: Write a short-answer question about the text on page 3 for each type of QAR. Then tell why the question represents that QAR.

Right There

Question **Answer** **Why this is a Right There QAR**

Think and Search

Question **Answer** **Why this is a Think and Search QAR**

Author and Me

Question **Answer** **Why this is an Author and Me QAR**

On My Own

Question **Answer** **Why this is an On My Own QAR**

Concept Lesson 1

Directions: Write four new questions about the text on page 3 in the spaces provided. (Do not fill in the answers.) When instructed to do so, exchange your *Student Activity Book* with a partner and answer each other's questions.

Partner's Name: _____

Directions: Answer each question, identify the QAR, and explain how you know what kind of QAR it is.

1.

   Answer:

   QAR:

   How do you know:

2.

   Answer:

   QAR:

   How do you know:

Concept Lesson 1

3.

Answer:

QAR:

How do you know:

4.

Answer:

QAR:

How do you know:

Directions: Read this passage from *Sue at the Field Museum*.

Sue the T-Rex

The first *T. rex* specimen was found in 1900. Since then, only seven skeletons that are more than half complete have been discovered. Of these, Sue is the largest, most complete, and best preserved *T. rex* ever found. Most of Sue's bones are in excellent condition and have a high degree of surface detail. Sixty-seven million years after her death, it is still possible to see fine details showing where muscles, tendons, and other soft tissues rested against or attached to the bone. Sue's completeness, combined with the exquisite preservation of the bones, makes her an invaluable scientific resource, permitting highly detailed study of *T. rex* anatomy.

In the summer of 1990, Sue Hendrickson was working as a fossil hunter with a commercial fossil-collecting team near Faith, South Dakota. On August 12 most of the team went into town to get a flat tire fixed and to take a short break from the heat. Sue stayed behind to look for fossils. She hiked over to some sandstone bluffs that had previously caught her attention. Within minutes she spotted some bone fragments on the ground. She scanned the cliffs above to find out where the fragments had fallen from and saw dinosaur bones—big ones. She climbed up the cliff for a better look at the bones, and saw they were huge. She thought she had found a *T. rex*, and when the team returned, they confirmed her find and promptly named it "Sue" in her honor.

Soon after Sue was discovered, her bones became the center of a dispute. Who owned the fossil?

To dig up dinosaurs, you always need the landowner's permission. But in Sue's case it was unclear whose land it was because . . . the bones were found on land that was part of a Sioux Indian reservation, BUT . . . the land belonged to a private rancher, BUT . . . the rancher was part Sioux, and his land was held in trust by the U.S. government. While people argued about who owned Sue, the bones were safely locked away in storerooms at the South Dakota School of Mines and Technology. In the end, a judge decided that Sue was held in trust by the U.S. government for the rancher on whose property the skeleton had been found. The rancher, in turn, decided to sell Sue at public auction.

Following the long custody battle, Sue was sold at Sotheby's auction house in New York on October 4, 1997. Just eight minutes after the bidding started, the Field Museum of Chicago purchased Sue for nearly $8.4 million—the most money ever paid for a fossil. On May 17, 2000, the Field Museum unveiled Sue, the largest, most complete, and best preserved *T. rex* fossil yet discovered.

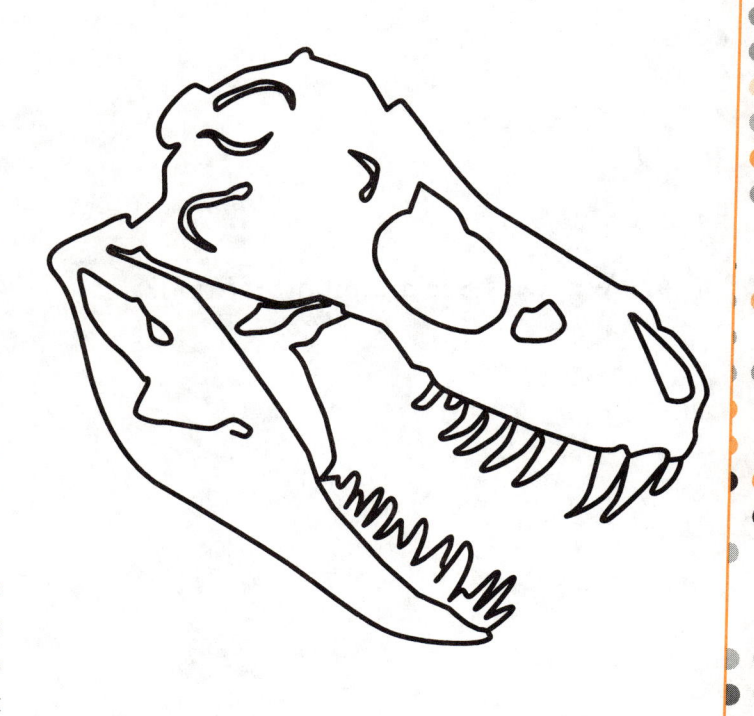

Directions: Answer the questions below about the text on page 11. Then, identify the text structure and the strategy you used to find the answer.

QUESTION / ANSWER

1. Who found Sue?
   - **A.** A rancher
   - **B.** A hike
   - **C.** A professional fossil hunter
   - **D.** None of the above

2. What happened after Sue was found?
   - **A.** The ownership of the bones was contested.
   - **B.** The bones were temporarily stored at a university.
   - **C.** The bones were put on display at a museum.
   - **D.** All of the above.

3. Why was the ownership of the bones unclear?

4. Why was Sue an important find?

TEXT STRUCTURE	STRATEGY
1.	1.
2.	2.
3.	3.
4.	4.

Concept Lesson 2

Directions: Write two short-answer Think and Search questions about the text on page 11. Then for each question, write the answer, identify the text structure, and tell why the QAR is Think and Search.

1.

   Answer:

   Text Structure:

   Why this is a Think and Search QAR:

2.

   Answer:

   Text Structure:

   Why this is a Think and Search QAR:

Directions: Write two new questions about the text on page 11 in the spaces provided. (Do not fill in the answers.) When instructed to do so, exchange your *Student Activity Book* with a partner and answer each other's questions.

Partner's Name: _____

Directions: Answer each question, identify the QAR, explain how you know what kind of QAR it is, and identify the strategies you used.

1.

   Answer:

   QAR:

   How do you know:

   Strategies for finding the answer:

2.

   Answer:

   QAR:

   How do you know:

   Strategies for finding the answer:

Concept Lesson 2

In My Head Sample Questions

1. **Author and Me: Text to Self**
   - How would you feel if you were the main character?
   - Compare your experience with that of someone in the story.
   - How does the situation today reflect the outcome of events described in the text?

   Notes:

2. **Author and Me: Text to Text**
   - Compare the main character with a character in another text you have read. How is he or she the same or different?

   Notes:

3. **Author and Me: Text to Themes**
   - What is the theme of the story?
   - What do you think was the author's primary message to the reader?

   Notes:

4. **On My Own**
   - Do you think women have full civil rights? Why or why not? Explain your conclusion.
   - Describe a time when you were scared. Why were you frightened? What happened?

   Notes:

Directions: Read this excerpt from *The Red Badge of Courage: An Episode of the American Civil War* by Stephen Crane. Then answer the questions on the next page.

The Red Badge of Courage

The cold passed reluctantly from the earth, and the retiring fogs revealed an army stretched out on the hills, resting. As the landscape changed from brown to green, the army awakened, and began to tremble with eagerness at the noise of rumors....

Once a certain tall soldier developed virtues and went resolutely to wash a shirt. He came flying back from a brook waving his garment bannerlike. He was swelled with a tale he had heard from a reliable friend, who had heard it from a truthful cavalryman, who had heard it from his trustworthy brother, one of the orderlies at division headquarters. He adopted the important air of a herald in red and gold. "We're goin' t' move t' morrah—sure," he said pompously to a group in the company street. "We're goin' 'way up the river, cut across, an' come around in behint 'em."

To his attentive audience he drew a loud and elaborate plan of a very brilliant campaign. When he had finished, the blue-clothed men scattered into small arguing groups between the rows of squat brown huts.... "It's a lie! that's all it is—a thunderin' lie!" said another private loudly. His smooth face was flushed, and his hands were thrust sulkily into his trousers' pockets. He took the matter as an affront to him. "I don't believe the derned old army's ever going to move. We're set. I've got ready to move eight times in the last two weeks, and we ain't moved yet."

The tall soldier felt called upon to defend the truth of a rumor he himself had introduced. He and the loud one came near to fighting over it....

Many of the men engaged in a spirited debate. One outlined in a peculiarly lucid manner all the plans of the commanding general. He was opposed by men who advocated that there were other plans of campaign. They clamored at each other, numbers making futile bids for the popular attention. Meanwhile, the soldier who had fetched the rumor bustled about with much importance....

There was a youthful private who listened with eager ears to the words of the tall soldier and to the varied comments of his comrades. After receiving a fill of discussions concerning marches and attacks, he went to his hut and crawled through an intricate hole that served it as a door. He wished to be alone with some new thoughts that had lately come to him....

The youth was in a little trance of astonishment. So they were at last going to fight. On the morrow, perhaps, there would be a battle, and he would be in it. For a time he was obliged to labor to make himself believe. He could not accept with assurance an omen that he was about to mingle in one of those great affairs of the earth.

He had, of course, dreamed of battles all his life—of vague and bloody conflicts that had thrilled him with their sweep and fire. In visions he had seen himself in many struggles. He had imagined peoples secure in the shadow of his eagle-eyed prowess. But awake he had regarded battles as crimson blotches on the pages of the past. He had put them as things of the bygone with his thought-images of heavy crowns and high castles. There was a portion of the world's history which he had regarded as the time of wars, but it, he thought, had been long gone over the horizon and had disappeared forever.

Directions: Answer the following questions about the text on page 17. Indicate the type of QAR, where you found the answer, and the strategies you used to find the answer.

QUESTION / ANSWER / QAR

1. Describe how the soldiers responded to the rumor of battle and how you react to rumors or gossip that you hear.

   QAR: _____

2. The "youth" in this passage "was about to mingle in one of those great affairs of the earth." Compare this "great affair" with an event in another story you have read.

   QAR: _____

3. In this passage, one of the author's themes is
   A. how the uncertainty of war affected the soldiers
   B. people will believe anything they hear
   C. the soldiers were not afraid to die
   D. the virtues of bravery

   QAR: _____

4. What would it be like to be a soldier facing battle? What would your thoughts and concerns be?

   QAR: _____

Concept Lesson 3

SOURCE	STRATEGY
1.	1.
2.	2.
3.	3.
4.	4.

Concept Lesson 3

Directions: Write two short-answer In My Head questions about the text on page 17. Then write the answers and why the QAR categories are In My Head.

Question	Answer	Why this is an In My Head QAR

Question	Answer	Why this is an In My Head QAR

Directions: Write two new questions about the text on page 17 in the spaces provided. (Do not fill in the answers.) When instructed to do so, exchange your *Student Activity Book* with a partner and answer each other's questions.

Partner's Name: _____

Directions: Answer each question, identify the QAR, and explain how you know what type of QAR it is.

1.

Answer:

QAR:

How do you know:

2.

Answer:

QAR:

How do you know:

Concept Lesson 3

Test-Taking Strategies

Before you read the text…

- Read the test questions first.
- Scan for key words in the text.
- Skim first and last sentences; read the text quickly to find the main idea.

As you read…

- Circle, underline, or highlight key words or phrases.
- Identify important information and make notes.
- Predict what will happen next.
- Connect to the text. Ask yourself: What do I already know about this topic? What else have I read about this topic? Have I experienced something similar?
- Identify the theme.

Before you answer the question…

- Reread the question.
- Identify the QAR.
- Reread or skim the text.
- Scan your notes and words or phrases that you highlighted in the text.
- Brainstorm an answer and briefly note your thoughts. For an essay question, make a short outline of your answer.

For your answer…

- Summarize, infer, draw conclusions, or make connections.
- Support your answer with details from the text.
- Write complete sentences. Use conventional grammar, punctuation, and spelling.
- Pace yourself. Don't spend too much time on any one answer.

Directions: Read the following excerpt from *Ellen Foster* by Kaye Gibbons.

Chapter 1, Part 1

When I was little I would think of ways to kill my daddy…

He drank his own self to death the year after the County moved me out… And I can say for a fact that I am better off now than when he was alive.

I live in a clean brick house and mostly I am left to myself. When I start to carry an odor I take a bath and folks tell me how sweet I look.

There is a plenty to eat here and if we run out of something we just go to the store and get some more. I had me a egg sandwich for breakfast, mayonnaise on both sides. And I may fix me another one for lunch.

Two years ago I did not have much of anything. Not that I live in the lap of luxury now but I am proud for the schoolbus to pick me up here every morning. My stylish well-groomed self standing in the front yard with the grass green and the hedge bushes square.

I figure I made out pretty good considering the rest of my family is either dead or crazy…

Oh but I do remember when I was scared. Everything was so wrong like somebody had knocked something loose and my family was shaking itself to death. Some wild ride broke and the one in charge strolled off and let us spin and shake and fly off the rail. And they both died tired of the wild crazy spinning and wore out and sick…

Even my mama's skin looked tired of holding in her weak self. She would prop herself up by the refrigerator and watch my daddy go round the table swearing at all who did him wrong. She looked all sad in her face like it was all her fault.

She comes home from the hospital sometimes. If I was her I would stay there. All laid up in the air conditioning with folks patting your head and bringing you fruit baskets.

Oh no. She comes in and he lets into her right away. Carrying on. Set up in his E-Z lounger like he is King for a Day. You bring me this or that he might say.

She comes in the door and he asks about supper right off. What does she have planned? he wants to know. Wouldn't he like to know what I myself have planned?… More like a big mean baby than a grown man…

Big wind-up toy of a man. He is just too sorry to talk back to even if he is my daddy. And she is too limp and too sore to get up the breath to push the words out to stop it all. She just stands there and lets him work out his evil on her.

Get in the kitchen and fix me something to eat. I had to cook the whole time you was gone, he tells her.

And that was some lie he made up. Cook for his own self. Ha. If I did not feed us both we had to go into town and get take-out chicken. I myself was looking forward to something fit to eat but I was not about to say anything.

Directions: Complete this chart as you work together with your peers and teacher.

QUESTION / ANSWER / QAR

1. The relationship Ellen had with her dad was that
   - A. he took care of her
   - B. she took care of him
   - C. she lived away from him
   - D. she admired him

   QAR: _____

2. What has happened to Ellen in the past two years?

   QAR: _____

3. Compare Ellen's old life with her new life.

   QAR: _____

4. What does Ellen value most in life?

   QAR: _____

STRATEGY

1.

2.

3.

4.

Directions: Read more from *Ellen Foster*. Then answer the questions on pages 27 through 29.

Chapter 1, Part 2

Nobody yells after anybody to do this or that here.

My new mama lays out the food and we all take a turn to dish it out. Then we eat and have a good time. Toast or biscuits with anything you please. Eggs any style. Corn cut off the cob the same day we eat it. I keep my elbows off the table and wipe my mouth like a lady. …When everybody is done eating my new mama puts the dishes in a thing, shuts the door, cuts on it, and Wa-La they are clean

My mama does not say a word about being tired or sore. She did ask who kept everything so clean and he took the credit. I do not know who he thinks he fooled. I knew he lied and my mama did too. She just asked to be saying something.

Mama puts the food out on the table and he wants to know what I am staring at. At you humped over your plate like one of us is about to snatch it from you. You old hog. But I do not say it.

Why don't you eat? he wants to know.

I don't have an appetite, I say back.

Well, you better eat. Your mama looks like this might be her last supper.

He is so sure he's funny that he laughs at his own self…

Now at my new mama's I lay up late in the day and watch the rain fall outside. Not one thing is pressing on me to get done here.

I have a bag of candy to eat on. One piece at a time. Make it last. All I got left to do is eat supper and wash myself.

Look around my room. It is so nice.

When I accumulate enough money I plan to get some colored glass things that you dangle from the window glass. I lay here and feature how that would look. I already got pink checkerboard curtains with dingleballs around the edges. My new mama sewed them for me. She also sewed matching sacks that I cram my pillows into every morning.

Everything matches. It is all so neat and clean…

The yelling makes my mama jump and if she was asleep she is awake now. Grits her teeth every time he calls out damn this or that. The more he drinks the less sense he makes.

By the time the dog races come on he's stretched out on the bathroom floor and can't get up. I know I need to go in there and poke him. Same thing every Saturday…

I get up and go in there and tell him to get up that folks got to come in here and do their business.

He can go lay in the truck.

He just grunts and grabs at my ankle and misses.

Get on up I say again to him. You got to be firm when he is like this. He'd lay there and rot if I let him so I nudge him with my foot. I will not touch my hands to him. Makes me want to heave my own self seeing him pull himself up on the sink. He zig-zags out through the living room and

Chapter 1, Part 2 (continued)

I guess he makes it out the door. I don't hear him fall down the steps.

And where did she come from? Standing in the door looking at it all.

Get back in bed, I say to mama.

Mama's easy to tend to. She goes back in the bedroom. Not a bit of trouble. Just stiff and hard to move around. I get her back in the bed and tell her he's outside for the night. She starts to whimper and I say it is no reason to cry. But she will wear herself out crying.

I ought to lock him out.

A grown man that should be bringing her food to nibble on and books to look at. No but he is taking care of his own self tonight. Just like she is not sick or kin to him.

A storm is coming up. And I will lay here with my mama until I see her chest rise up and sink down regular. Deep and regular and far away from the man in the truck.

Directions: Answer the questions below and on the next two pages. Identify the QAR categories and the test-taking strategies you used.

1. Ellen is most upset that her father

    A. doesn't work

    B. abuses her mother

    C. does not take care of her mother

    D. does not take care of her

    QAR: _____

    Test-Taking Strategy:

2. Describe Ellen's feelings toward her father during the scene when her mother has returned home.

    QAR: _____

    Test-Taking Strategy:

3. What role has Ellen taken on in her birth family and why?

   QAR: _____
   Test-Taking Strategy:

4. Ellen's feelings toward her father could best be described as
   A. anger
   B. pity
   C. disgust
   D. A and B
   E. A and C
   QAR: _____
   Test-Taking Strategy:

5. Describe the stability and simple pleasures of Ellen's new life.

   QAR: _____
   Test-Taking Strategy:

6. If Ellen went to your school, what would you think of her? Give specific examples and reasons.

   QAR: _____
   Test-Taking Strategy:

7. Ellen's new life is like her old one because
   A. no one yells
   B. her mother takes care of her
   C. she has plenty to eat
   D. she lives in a messy place
   E. none of the above

   QAR: _____
   Test-Taking Strategy:

8. How does Ellen's birth mother react to her husband?

   QAR: _____
   Test-Taking Strategy:

9. Compare and contrast Ellen's new life with her old life. Use details from the story to support your answer.

   QAR: _____
   Test-Taking Strategy:

10. Ellen had to struggle to survive in her birth family. Describe a personal experience in which you struggled for success, happiness, stability, approval, or some other goal.

    QAR: _____
    Test-Taking Strategy:

Directions: Read the following article by Marcella J. Kehus.

The Complexities of Cloning

Before 1996, few people had actually considered cloning a real possibility beyond something you might read about or see in a science fiction movie. But in July of that year, when Dolly the ewe (baby sheep) was born as a clone of her mother, some great debates began that are still raging in many areas. Cloning, or the creating of a living replica from DNA from a body cell, took quite a long time to develop before it actually worked with Dolly as its first success. Now people from politicians to religious leaders to scientists and the general public continue to argue over whether this technology should be applied to humans. The basic debate comes down to: Should we or should we not allow the cloning of human beings? And, if we do so, what are the possible results?

Now that the procedure for cloning has been discovered, it seems only a matter of time before it is applied to humans. This is where a number of people, specialists and general citizens alike, have serious concerns. One of their primary concerns, which often comes up with every new technology, are the number of ways that such a technology might be abused. For example, what if a certain group wanted to use cloning to create an army of exact duplicate soldiers or creatures to carry out their evil deeds? And, because cloning can include genetic engineering, or selecting just the right genes to create a certain kind of being (strong, green eyes, etc.), the idea of creating a look-alike super-human race reminds people quickly of the terrible possibilities of Hitler-like beliefs if given the power of cloning.

There are lesser kinds of abuses that the power of human cloning could inspire. Perhaps a former football player got his career cut short due to an injury; what would keep him from creating a clone of himself to play and become the star he always wanted to be? Cloning could become a fashionable way for other conceited people to just re-create themselves and the result may be a child who is never given a chance to become an individual.

On the other hand, there are impressive possibilities when it comes to human cloning. First, cloning is another possible solution for couples who are otherwise unable to have children of their own. In fact, the medical solutions made possible by clones are numerous including the supplying of life-saving transplant organs or bone marrow by cloned family members that would automatically match. And, when coupled with genetic engineering, cloning may allow us to create better humans as we discover more and more about disease and aging and produce clones who are better-equipped to survive.

Certainly, the possibilities of human cloning are scientifically possible. Yet, as with other new developments, one must carefully consider the possible outcomes—both good and bad. Ultimately, we as a society will make the decision as to whether human cloning's benefits outweigh its possible abuses and where we go from here.

Directions: Answer the following questions about the article on page 30 and identify each QAR.

1. According to the article, what "great debate" started in 1996?

   QAR: _____

2. What are other arguments against cloning that are not mentioned in the article?

   QAR: _____

3. Who is involved in the debate about human cloning?

   QAR: _____

4. What do you think is the strongest reason given for human cloning? Why?

   QAR: _____

Concept Lesson 5

5. What do you think is the strongest reason against human cloning? Why?

   QAR: _____

6. What are three different ways that individuals might benefit from human cloning?

   QAR: _____

7. Who do you think will make the final decision about whether or not human cloning is allowed?

   QAR: _____

Essay-Writing Tips, Part 1

- Before you start writing, identify the QAR.

- Create a short outline of your main thesis or idea and two or three main points that support your thesis. If you're stuck, do some brainstorming.

- Restate the question as a thesis or opening line(s).

- Answer all parts of the question. Check off each part as you go.

- For each part of the answer, note the specific part in the text that supports it.

- Include an introduction, at least two body paragraphs, and a conclusion.

- Present your ideas in a logical way. What comes first, second, third? What is your conclusion?

- If you have time, reread your essay to correct spelling, punctuation, or grammatical errors.

Directions: Reread the passage on page 30. Then choose a side for or against human cloning and write an essay to convince your audience to believe as you do.

Directions: Read "The Bungee Lunge" on pages 36 and 37. As you read, write five during reading questions in the spaces below. Identify the QAR that each question represents.

1.

   QAR: _____

2.

   QAR: _____

3.

   QAR: _____

4.

   QAR: _____

5.

   QAR: _____

Directions: Read this article by Karen McNulty.

The Bungee Lunge

Here's your giant rubber band. Now jump! It's only a 10-story plunge—and science will spring you back.

The Science Behind the Bounce

Ready?

When standing high on a jump platform, you have lots of potential (stored) energy.

Jump!

Leap off and your potential energy is converted to kinetic energy, the energy of motion. For a few seconds, you experience free fall, until there's no more slack in the cord.

Stret – t – ch

Then the cord starts to stretch. This stores the energy of your fall in the cord.

Bounce

This stored energy springs you back up. You fall and bounce again… and again…

Phew!

Each bounce disperses some of your energy, so eventually you stop. You'll have to hang around until someone lowers you to a raft or the ground.

You're hanging onto the railing of a bridge, 46 m above the river. Your friends on the bank below seem awfully small; looking at them makes you dizzy. Someone standing behind you is counting down "Three…two…one!" Defying every sane notion in your brain, you leap—headfirst.

The 100 km/h fall toward the water terrifies you. But just as you close your eyes for the icy plunge, something happens: You bounce back!

Better thank your lucky *bungee cord*—that wrist-thick band of latex rubber strapped to your ankles and anchored to the bridge. Because it was the right length, it kept you high and dry. And because it stret-t-t-ched and recoiled—giving you a few good bounces—it used up the energy of your fall so you didn't get torn limb from limb. Phew!

Those who have done it say it's the thrill of a lifetime—"a natural high." Others call it crazy. But everyone knows it as "bungee jumping," the sport springing up (and down) across the nation.

At least one group of people has been "bungee jumping" for ages: the men of Pentecost Island in the South Pacific. They make cords from elastic vines, lash them to their ankles, and plunge off wooden towers into pits of softened earth. For these islanders, jumping is a springtime ritual, meant to demonstrate courage and supposedly ensure a plentiful yam harvest.

In North America, jumpers take the bungee plunge just for the excitement of it. Scott Bergman, who runs a bungee-jumping company in California, explains the appeal. "It's a feeling of having absolutely no control—and loving it."

And it doesn't take any skill. Just $75 to $100 and *faith*—in physics. It's a simple physics equation, after all, that let's "jump masters" like Bergman determine how far the cord will stretch when you take the plunge—whether it will stretch too far.

The Bungee Lunge (continued)

Weighing the Odds

The major variables are the stretchiness, or *elasticity*, of the cord—predetermined by the manufacturer—and the jumper's weight. As you might guess, "the heavier you are, the more the cord is going to stretch," says physicist Peter Brancazio.

By weighing customers (they don't just ask), using the equation, and adjusting cords, jump masters have bounced thousands to safety. (There have been some deaths—usually caused by frayed cords or other faulty equipment.)

Jump experts can even adjust the cords to give their clients custom-made thrills. "When we jump off bridges in California," says Bergman, "we ask the people if they want to just touch the water, dunk their heads in, or go all the way. We can really get it that exact."

Really? "I wouldn't trust them," says Brancazio, "but I guess they can."

If, for example, Bergman calculates that you'll crack your skull on a rock in the river, he can shorten your cord. "That starts the stretch at a higher point off the ground," says Brancazio.

Or you can jump with two cords. "In that case," says Brancazio, your weight is "equally divided between the cords so each stretches half as far."

Chances are, you'll scream just as hard with fear and delight.

Directions: Write a short answer to the following questions based on the article on pages 36 and 37 and identify the QAR for each.

1. Explain how energy is stored and released in a bungee cord.

   QAR: _____

2. Summarize the points of view of the two experts (Scott Bergman and Peter Brancazio) quoted in the article. Why might they have different perspectives on bungee jumping?

   QAR: _____

3. Would you ever consider bungee jumping? What would be your major considerations in making a decision?

   QAR: _____

4. Compare bungee jumping in the South Pacific to California.

   QAR: _____

5. Compare the during reading questions you wrote on page 35 with the questions above. What types of QAR categories are there? Which of your questions prepared you for the questions asked above, if any?

   QAR: _____

Booster Lesson 1

Tips for Using Textbooks

Look at text features:

- Headings and subheadings
- Summaries (main idea, key points)
- Terms and their definitions
- Words bolded or highlighted in the text
- Captions for illustrations

Use previewing techniques:

- Preview comprehension questions or exercises at the end.
- Skim the first and last sentences of each paragraph.

Take notes and ask questions:

- Restate definitions and explanations in your own words.
- Connect to the text: What do I already know? What do I want to learn?
- Restate or paraphrase questions in your own words.

Directions: Read this passage from *American History: The Early Years to 1877.*

The Women's Rights Movement

Guide to Reading

Main Idea

Emboldened by their work in the antislavery movement, many women fought to improve their own status in society.

Read to Learn...

* why women became unhappy with their positions in the mid-1800s
* how working in the antislavery movement prepared women to fight for their own rights
* what arguments opponents used against the women's rights movement

Terms to Know

* abolitionist
* suffrage

Women took a special interest in the antislavery movement. As they fought for social reform for African Americans, they realized that they also lacked full social and political rights. When women such as Angelina and Sarah Grimké tried to participate actively in the antislavery movement, they often met resistance. As a result, many abolitionists became crusaders for women's rights.

Equal rights for women would require major reform. In the 1800s women actually had fewer rights than in colonial times. They had few political or legal rights. Women could not vote. They could not hold public office. A woman's husband owned all her property.

Antislavery Movement Gives Women a Boost

Women from New England to Ohio joined the antislavery societies. They worked hard, gathering signatures on thousands of petitions to send to Congress. They also read about and discussed the abuses of slavery. Many saw similarities between the treatment of enslaved persons and women.

In her book *Woman in the Nineteenth Century,* journalist **Margaret Fuller** observed that "there exists in the minds of men a tone of feeling toward women as towards slaves." Abolitionists Angelina and Sarah Grimké confronted this feeling when they spoke to antislavery groups. Audiences did not criticize their stand on slavery. They did, though, question their right to speak in public.

As a result, the Grimkés soon found themselves in the midst of "an entirely new contest—a contest for the rights of woman." Sarah wrote that "all I ask… is that [men] will take their feet from off our necks and permit us to stand upright."

The Women's Rights Movement

Their involvement in the antislavery movement and other reform movements gave women roles outside their homes and families. They learned valuable skills, such as organizing, working

The Women's Rights Movement (continued)

together, and speaking in public. Eventually they used these skills to further their own cause—the women's rights movement.

In 1840 nine women from the United States attended the World Anti-Slavery Convention in **London**. When the women arrived at the convention, however, the male delegates barred them from participating. The women and some male allies protested. On the first day of the convention, delegates debated the situation.

Clergy at the convention considered it improper for women to participate. Other male delegates declared women "unfit for public or business meetings." In the end, the majority of delegates decided that women could not take part in discussions. Instead, the women delegates would have to sit in the gallery behind a curtain.

Humiliated and angry, two of the women, Lucretia Coffin Mott and Elizabeth Cady Stanton, spent hours after the meetings talking about women's position in society. They realized that they could not bring about social change if they themselves lacked social and political rights. Stanton and Mott "resolved to hold a convention as soon as we returned home, and form a society to advocate the rights of women."

The Seneca Falls Convention

Eight years passed before the two friends organized their convention. On July 19, 1848, the first women's rights convention opened in Seneca Falls, New York. Both male and female delegates attended the convention. The delegates issued the Seneca Falls Declaration, which proclaimed that "all men and women are created equal."

Then the declaration listed several resolutions. One of them demanded suffrage, or the right to vote, for women. Even supporters of women's rights hesitated to pass this bold demand. Mott exclaimed, "Oh, Lizzie, thou will make us ridiculous! We must go slowly." But Stanton refused to withdraw the resolution. After much heated debate, it passed by a narrow margin.

The Seneca Falls Convention marked the beginning of an organized women's rights movement. Following the convention, women did not achieve all of their demands. They did, however, overcome some obstacles. Many states passed laws permitting women to own their own property and keep their earnings. Many men and women, though, continued to oppose the movement. Most politicians ignored or acted hostile to the issue of women's rights.

The Women's Rights Movement (continued)

Assessment

Check for Understanding
1. Define suffrage.
2. Why did women become unhappy with their position in the mid-1800s? About what areas of their daily lives were they most concerned?

Critical Thinking
3. **Comparing and Contrasting.** Contrast the views of the men and women who opposed the women's rights movement with those who supported it.

4. **Identifying Relationships.** Re-create the diagram shown here, and list how women's work in the antislavery movement prepared them to fight for their own rights.

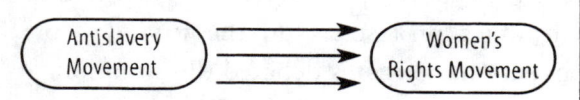

Antislavery Movement → Women's Rights Movement

Interdisciplinary Activity

5. **Citizenship.** Are women today denied any rights that men have? Draw up an agenda for a new Seneca Falls Convention listing topics for discussion.

Directions: Read "The Women's Rights Movement" on pages 40 and 41 and answer the questions from the Assessment section on page 42. Identify the type of QAR each question represents.

1.

   QAR: _____

2.

   QAR: _____

3.

   QAR: _____

4.

   QAR: _____

5.

Write your agenda on a separate sheet or in your "QAR Reflections Journal."

   QAR: _____

Booster Lesson 2

Directions: Read this letter to President Franklin D. Roosevelt.

Dear Mr. President

Phila., Pa.
November 26, 1934

Honorable Franklin D. Roosevelt
Washington, D.C.

Dear Mr. President:

I am forced to write to you because we find ourselves in a very serious condition. For the last three or four years we have had depression and suffered with my family and little children severely. Now Since the Home Owners Loan Corporation opened up, I have been going up there in order to save my home, because there has been unemployment in my house for more than three years. You can imagine that I and my family have suffered from lack of water supply in my house for more than two years. Last winter I did not have coal and the pipes burst in my house and therefore could not make heat in the house. Now winter is here again and we are suffering of cold, no water in the house, and we are facing to be forced out of the house, because I have no money to move or pay so much money as they want when after making settlement. I am mother of little children, am sick and losing my health, and we are eight people in the family, and where can I go when I don't have money because no one is working in my house. The Home Loan Corporation wants $42. a month rent or else we will have to be on the street. I am living in this house for about ten years and when times were good we would put our last cent in the house and now I have no money, no home and no wheres to go. I beg of you to please help me and my family and little children for the sake of a sick mother and a suffering family to give this your immediate attention so we will not be forced to move or put out in the street.

Waiting and Hoping that you will act quickly.
Thanking you very much I remain

Mrs. E. L.

Directions: Read this excerpt from a speech by Robert Kennedy.

On the Death of Dr. Martin Luther King

This speech was given by Robert F. Kennedy on April 4, 1968, shortly after Dr. Martin Luther King, Jr. had been assassinated. At the time, Robert Kennedy was a U.S. Senator leading a race for the presidency, but he was assassinated a few months later.

Martin Luther King dedicated his life to love and to justice between fellow human beings. He died in the cause of that effort. In this difficult day, in this difficult time for the United States, it's perhaps well to ask what kind of a nation we are and what direction we want to move in.

For those of you who are black—considering the evidence evidently is that there were white people who were responsible—you can be filled with bitterness, and with hatred, and a desire for revenge.

We can move in that direction as a country, in greater polarization—black people amongst blacks, and white amongst whites, filled with hatred toward one another. Or we can make an effort, as Martin Luther King did, to understand and to comprehend, and replace that violence, that stain of bloodshed that has spread across our land, with an effort to understand, compassion and love.

For those of you who are black and are tempted to be filled with hatred and mistrust of the injustice of such an act, against all white people, I would only say that I can also feel in my own heart the same kind of feeling. I had a member of my family killed, but he was killed by a white man.

But we have to make an effort in the United States, we have to make an effort to understand, to get beyond these rather difficult times.

My favorite poet was Aeschylus. He once wrote: "Even in our sleep, pain which cannot forget falls drop by drop upon the heart, until, in our own despair, against our will, comes wisdom through the awful grace of God."

What we need in the United States is not division; what we need in the United States is not hatred; what we need in the United States is not violence and lawlessness, but is love and wisdom, and compassion toward one another, and a feeling of justice toward those who still suffer within our country, whether they be white or whether they be black.

So I ask you tonight to return home, to say a prayer for the family of Martin Luther King, yeah that's true, but more importantly to say a prayer for our own country, which all of us love—a prayer for understanding and that compassion of which I spoke. We can do well in this country. We will have difficult times. We've had difficult times in the past. And we will have difficult times in the future. It is not the end of violence; it is not the end of lawlessness; and it's not the end of disorder.

But the vast majority of white people and the vast majority of black people in this country want to live together, want to improve the quality of our life, and want justice for all human beings that abide in our land.

Let us dedicate ourselves to what the Greeks wrote so many years ago: to tame the savageness of man and make gentle the life of this world.

Let us dedicate ourselves to that, and say a prayer for our country and for our people.

Directions: Read pages 44 and 45 and then answer the following questions. Identify the QAR after your answer.

1. Compare and contrast the audience, purpose, and writing style of the two passages.

   QAR: _____

2. If you were President Roosevelt, how would you have responded to Mrs. E. L.'s letter? Why?

   QAR: _____

3. What would have been your reaction to Robert F. Kennedy's speech at the time. Why?

   QAR: _____

Best-Answer Strategies

IN THE BOOK

Right There
- Reread.
- Scan for key words.
- Recall key facts or figures.

Think and Search
- Reread.
- Scan for key words.
- Skim first and last sentences.
- Identify important information.
- Look for specific examples.
- Identify characters or people, events, plot, problem and solutions, etc.
- Identify the main idea or theme.
- Predict what will happen next.

IN MY HEAD

Author and Me
- Reread.
- Skim first and last sentences.
- Connect to important information. What do I already know about this subject?
- Connect to the characters or people and events in the text.
- Connect to the main idea or theme.
- Predict what will happen next.
- Connect to other texts. What have I read before on this same subject or with this same theme?

On My Own
- Reread.
- Connect to the general theme or topic.
- Connect to other texts. What have I read before on this same subject or with this same theme?

Directions: Read this passage from *Lasers* by Lynne Kelly and answer the questions on page 49.

How a Laser Beam Is Made

The first pulse laser was made by Theodore H. Maiman of the United States in 1960. He used a ruby rod to make a short flash of laser light. The method has been improved since then, but the idea is the same.

1. A rod of ruby, about the size of a finger is used. Real ruby is very expensive, but synthetic ruby can be used.

2. The ends of the ruby rod are ground so they are perfectly smooth and parallel to each other. Each end is painted silver to make mirrors, but one end receives a thinner layer of paint than the other. This means that this end is only partially reflective.

3. A flash tube is wrapped around the ruby rob and connected to a battery. The flash tube and battery act as the power source.

4. When the flash tube is switched on, it produces bright, white light. This excites, or increases, the energy level of chromium atoms in the ruby. Light is reflected back and forth along the rod.

5. After a fraction of a second, a bright flash of red laser light will come out of the end of the ruby rod.

When the flash tube is switched on, chromium atoms in the ruby rod absorb some of the light energy. These atoms then give out energy again in the form of colored light. Light beams given out from one sort of atom that has been excited in this way will all be identical.

These identical light beams reflect back and forth along the ruby rod from one mirror to the other. As they do so, they excite more atoms, which give off more light. This goes on until the light beam has grown strong enough to break through the thinner mirror. All the light beams emitted from the thinner mirror will be identical and coherent and will travel in a straight line. They will be a laser beam.

The name *laser* comes from the way in which a laser beam is made. It is a form of light that is the result of many reflections between the mirrors on the ends of the ruby rod. This causes the energy to increase, or amplify. The chromium atoms that give off the pure light beam have been excited, or stimulated, by the flash of light. The atoms give out, or emit, pure monochromatic light, which is a form of electromagnetic radiation.

So a laser beam is the result of **L**ight **A**mplification by **S**timulated **E**mission of **R**adiation.

Directions: Answer the following questions about the text on page 48.

1. Which list includes the items used in generating laser light?
   A. ruby rod, flash tube, light switch
   B. synthetic ruby, mirrors, chromium atoms
   C. ruby rod, flash tube, battery
   D. ruby rod, reflective coating, flash tube, battery

2. What is the purpose of the mirrors at each end of the rod?
   A. They intensify the energy of the light beams as the light beams reflect back and forth between the mirrors.
   B. The protect the ends of the ruby rod as the high energy light beams travel back and forth.
   C. They decrease the level of energy of the chromium atoms in the ruby.
   D. None of the above.

3. What is the purpose of the flash tube and battery?
   A. They hold the ruby rod in place.
   B. They excite the chromium atoms.
   C. They make the light beams coherent.
   D. They generate the power needed to produce the energy for the laser beam.

4. How is a laser beam made?

5. Choose question 1, 2, or 3 above and analyze each response (A, B, C, D). Is it correct, partially correct, or incorrect? Why? Identify a statement or section of the passage that supports your answer.

Booster Lesson 4

The Road Not Taken

Two roads diverged in a yellow wood,
And sorry I could not travel both
And be one traveler, long I stood
And looked down one as far as I could
To where it bent in the undergrowth;

Then took the other, as just as fair,
And having perhaps the better claim,
Because it was grassy and wanted wear;
Though as for that the passing there
Had worn them really about the same,

And both that morning equally lay
In leaves no step had trodden black.
Oh, I kept the first for another day!
Yet knowing how way leads on to way,
I doubted if I should ever come back.

I shall be telling this with a sigh
Somewhere ages and ages hence:
Two roads diverged in a wood, and I—
I took the one less traveled by,
And that has made all the difference.

by Robert Frost

Life

They told me that Life could be just what I made it—
    Life could be fashioned and worn like a gown;
I, the designer; mine the decision
    Whether to wear it with bonnet or crown.

And so I selected the prettiest pattern—
    Life should be made of the rosiest hue—
Something unique, and a bit out of fashion,
    One that perhaps would be chosen by few.

But other folks came and they leaned o'er my shoulder;
    Somebody questioned the ultimate cost;
Somebody tangled the thread I was using;
    One day I found that my scissors were lost.

And somebody claimed the material faded;
    Somebody said I'd be tired ere 'twas worn;
Somebody's fingers, too pointed and spiteful,
    Snatched at the cloth, and I saw it was torn.

Oh! somebody tried to do all the sewing,
    Wanting always to advise or condone.
Here is my life, the product of many;
    Where is that gown I could fashion—alone?

by Nan Terrell Reed

Directions: This test has two parts. When you're finished with Part 1, go on to Part 2.

Part 1

Directions: Read the poems on page 50 and 51. Then write five Author and Me questions (connecting self to text, text to text, and text to theme) about the poems.

Author and Me Questions
for "The Road Not Taken"

1.

2.

3.

4.

5.

Author and Me Questions
for "Life"

1.

2.

3.

4.

5.

Booster Lesson 5

Part 2

Directions: Answer the following questions about the two poems. Support your answers with details from the text. Identify the QAR after each answer.

1. In "The Road Not Taken," how did the narrator know that one of the roads was "less traveled by"?

   QAR: _____

2. Why did the narrator choose "the road less traveled by"?

   QAR: _____

3. How does the narrator feel about his decision?

   QAR: _____

Part 2, continued

4. What is the main idea or theme of "The Road Not Taken"?

   QAR: _____

5. In the poem "Life," what does the author compare life to? What did she want her life to be like?

   QAR: _____

6. Who is the "Somebody" referred to in the poem? What does this somebody do?

   QAR: _____

7. At the end of "Life," how does the narrator feel about her life?

   QAR: _____

Part 2, continued

8. What is the main idea or theme of "Life"?

   QAR: _____

9. Compare and contrast the narrators of the poems "The Road Not Taken" and "Life." What were they seeking? How did they feel about their "road taken" and "gown" at the end?

   QAR: _____

10. Compare and contrast the main ideas or themes in each poem. How are they different? How are they similar?

    QAR: _____

Booster Lesson 5

Solving Math Story Problems

Ask yourself...

1. **What is given?**

   Identify the information already stated or given in the problem.

2. **What am I supposed to figure out?**

   Restate the problem in terms of the unknown quantity.

3. **What is the math concept?**

   Identify the math concept or concepts you have to know. What have you already learned about this concept?

Do the work...

4. Set up the problem.

5. Do the calculation.

6. Select or write your answer.

> Always show your work. If you get an incorrect answer because of a computation error, you may get partial credit for setting up the problem correctly and showing how you got the answer.

Booster Lesson 6

Directions: Answer the following question. Refer to the steps on page 56 if necessary.

In Malia's eighth-grade class, 3 out of 5 students are girls. In a class of 30 students, how many are girls?

A. 12
B. 18
C. 20
D. 22

1. What is given?

2. What am I supposed to figure out?

3. What is the math concept?

4. Set up the problem.

5. Do the calculation.

6. Select or write your answer.

Booster Lesson 6

Essay-Writing Tips, Part 2

Purpose

Identify the purpose of the essay:
- Narration
- Information
- Persuasion

Audience

Identify who you are writing for.

Text Type

Identify the text type:
- Formal essay
- Letter
- Editorial
- Newspaper or journal article
- Procedure
- Others

Evaluation

- **Development:** Are the ideas well developed? Does the essay have good supporting or descriptive details?
- **Organization:** Is the essay well organized? Does it have good transitions between ideas and paragraphs?
- **Use of language:** Is the sentence structure varied? Is descriptive or figurative language used effectively?
- **Mechanics:** Do grammatical, spelling, and punctuation errors interfere with understanding the content?

Directions: Complete this worksheet as you work together with your peers and teacher.

ESSAY-WRITING WORKSHEET

Write an article for the school newspaper explaining the benefits of playing computer games.

QAR:

Purpose:

Audience:

Text Type:

Brainstorm Ideas:

Outline:

Directions: With a partner, complete the worksheet. Then write your letter on the next page.

ESSAY-WRITING WORKSHEET

Think of a social issue affecting your school, neighborhood, or community (for example, pollution, noise, litter, homelessness, traffic, etc.). Write a letter to a public official describing the problem and asking for help. Explain what you think should be done to solve it and why.

QAR:

Purpose:

Audience:

Text Type:

Brainstorm Ideas:

Outline:

Directions: Use this page to write your letter.

Booster Lesson 7

Directions: Complete this worksheet and write your essay on the next page.

ESSAY-WRITING WORKSHEET

Imagine that you just saw on the news that computer scientists have perfected the technologies behind artificial intelligence and expect manufacturers to begin making robots soon with many—but not all—human capabilities.

Explain what you and your family members would like robots to do if you could buy them. What kinds of things do you think the robots should or should not do?

QAR:

Purpose:

Audience:

Text Type:

Brainstorm Ideas:

Outline:

Booster Lesson 7

Directions: Use this page to write your essay.

Directions: Read the following article from *Teen Vogue,* as told to Sarah Brown by Bess Judson. Then answer the questions on pages 66 through 69.

Survivor

I noticed the bump during the summer. I thought it was cool the way it moved when I swallowed, like a seed sliding under the skin of an orange slice. I made my mom touch it. "Maybe it's a tumor!" I said, laughing. "It's probably just a swollen gland or something. We'll get it checked out if it doesn't go away soon," she said, and sent me off to school.

I was psyched to go to college... My first semester at Hamilton, in upstate New York, was so much fun. I joined the rugby team and started feeling really good about myself again.

I didn't even think about my bump until Christmas break, when I switched from a pediatrician to a general practitioner, who gave me a complete physical. As soon as she felt the lump on my thyroid she sent me for a needle biopsy. I thought it was routine, although I was surprised I went for tests right away, instead of having to schedule an appointment.

And then I went back to school. The first night I was back, my doctor called. The tumor was malignant. I had cancer, and in one week, I was scheduled to have an operation to remove my thyroid. I hung up the phone thinking back to the pink fluid the doctor had removed from my bump during the biopsy. The liquid had looked so harmless inside the syringe, like water used to clean a red paintbrush.

I was totally petrified. As soon as you hear that word—*cancer*—no one knows what to say. Doctors don't really even know that much about it. All they can do is try to cut it out.

My surgeon told me I'd need to take two weeks off from school, which is what I'd planned to do. I spent two nights in the hospital, in and out of sleep. Every few hours a man who called himself the Vampire would wake me up to draw my blood. When I finally stood up to walk, I had to hold my mother's arm to stay on my feet. I inched through the halls, rolling my IV beside me like a fish dragging the rod that hooked it....

Your thyroid is a gland in your neck—the part of your body that regulates metabolism (the physical and chemical processes that essentially maintain life). It also controls a lot of your hormones, and for about a month, I was just miserable. After surgery, I had to wait awhile before I could start taking thyroid-replacement hormones (which simulate the way an actual thyroid works), so my entire hormonal makeup was out of whack. I was tired and I was sad and I would cry all the time about nothing. I was what they call hypothyroid—I felt sluggish and just really crummy.

When I was finally allowed to start taking Synthroid (synthetic thyroid hormones), I was expecting to feel normal right away—to go back to classes and to play rugby in the spring. They have to raise the hormones to the right levels incrementally, so in the beginning, I was taking only about half the level I am now. I went back to school, and I did play rugby, but let's just say I wasn't a huge success. I was so much slower than I'd been before. My friends were totally supportive—they couldn't believe I was playing at all. I signed up for a full course load, but I ended up having to drop a class. In the fall semester, I'd gotten some C's and a D... but this time, somehow, I got straight A's. I think I was just happy to be back, happy I was able to pull through and rebound...

Survivor (continued)

I spent the spring and summer of my junior year studying in Spain. Seeing a different side of life—a side I'd never been exposed to before—gave me a new sense of perspective and taught me not to take so much for granted. When I got back, I knew I wanted to keep learning Spanish—to become fluent to the level of a native speaker, and to do something to help people along the way, if I could.... I had always thought about joining the Peace Corps, but I was never sure I could actually do it...

By my senior year, the more I thought about all the things I'd done, the more I knew that this time, I was strong enough to handle an experience like the Peace Corps. The hardest parts of my life have made me feel the most whole and the proudest of myself. I guess I needed to beat cancer to find out that I can do anything.

Directions: Answer the following questions about the article "Survivor."

1. The subject of "Survivor" was diagnosed with
    A. cancer of the blood (leukemia)
    B. cancer of the thyroid
    C. cancer of the throat
    D. hyperthyroidism
    E. none of the above

2. The thyroid works to regulate your metabolism or
    A. speed of body processes
    B. growth over a lifetime
    C. organ functions
    D. fighting off of disease
    E. none of the above

3. A *biopsy* is
    A. a gland in your neck
    B. a complete physical exam
    C. a procedure to extract blood or tissue from the body for analysis
    D. a drug that regulates your hormones
    E. a needle

4. Some of the symptoms of hypothyroidism are
    A. low energy
    B. depression or sadness
    C. sleeplessness
    D. A and B
    E. A and C

5. Thyroid replacement hormones
    A. cause hormonal imbalance
    B. are called Synthroid
    C. make you feel tired
    D. are effective right away
    E. simulate the way the thyroid works

6. Describe the events in Bess's life leading up to her decision to go into the Peace Corps.

7. Describe how Bess's battle with cancer affected her physically and emotionally. How was her academic and social life affected?

8. How did Bess feel about her experience with cancer?

9. Write an essay describing an experience in which you, someone you know, or a person or character you have read about was a "survivor." What was the experience? How did you or that person or character handle the experience? What were its impacts? What did the experience teach you (or the person or character)?

10. The Peace Corps is a government agency that sends volunteers to developing countries to assist communities in setting up businesses, to teach English, to train health care workers, to plant trees, and to do many other activities depending on the needs of the host country.

Write a letter of application to join the Peace Corps as if you were Bess Judson of "Survivor." Describe why you are a good candidate and the reasons they should accept your application.

QAR
Reflections Journal

_____
_____
_____
_____
_____

QAR Reflections Journal

QAR Reflections Journal